Why Are You Here?

The Spiritual Reality that Reveals Your Purpose in Life

Ian Todd

Print ISBN 978-1-948609-68-5
Ebook ISBN 978-1-948609-70-8

Printed in the United States of America

Library of Congress Cataloguing-in-Publication Data

Why Are You Here? The Spiritual Reality that Reveals Your Purpose in Life / Ian Todd

Acknowledgments

I thank God—and all the people throughout my life—who have inspired my journey of faith that has led to the writing of this book. I wish to acknowledge the theologians Thomas Jay Oord, Keith Ward and Alister McGrath (amongst others) whose writings have helped to clarify greatly my understanding of the nature of God and our relationship with God. I am grateful to all who have read and commented on drafts of this book, which has helped and encouraged me in bringing it to fruition. I thank my wife, Sue, for her constant support, and for the love that we share.

Dedication

To my wife Sue,
my children Catherine and Adam,
and my grandchildren Megan, Ella,
George, Mione, Oakley and Aubree.

Thank you for showing me the
true meaning of love.

Table of Contents

PART 1

PART 2

PART 1

Introduction

Two important types of questions we can ask about ourselves begin with either 'How?' or 'Why?'.

As a teenager, I was fascinated by Human Biology and the question 'How do our bodies work?' This led me to study Biochemistry as an undergraduate at university, and then to undertake PhD research in Immunology. I was then fortunate to have an academic career that involved teaching and research in Immunology—a subject I love.

What particularly fascinates me about Immunology is that it concerns understanding how molecules and cells of our bodies interact with each other, and also interact with microbes and other infectious agents, in order to defend our bodies against infection (that is, generate immunity).

This raises lots of 'How?' questions, the broadest of which is "How does the immune system work?" Indeed, the COVID-19 pandemic led many people who, hitherto, probably gave little or no thought to such matters, to ask very pertinent immunological questions, such as "How do vaccines work to protect me against the COVID-19 virus?"

So, answering these particular 'How?' questions about ourselves comes down to understanding the structures and functions of the materials that are the building blocks of our bodies.

On the other hand, however much we understand about the materials that constitute our incredibly complex bodies, that knowledge can never answer some of the most funda-mental 'Why?' questions we might ask about ourselves.

Perhaps *the* most fundamental question we can ask about ourselves is, 'Why do we exist?'

All that Biology can tell is 'How we exist', not 'Why we exist'. Or, if we try to answer the 'Why?' question using Biology alone, the answer would be something like, "We exist in order to reproduce before we die, thereby to gen-erate similar versions of ourselves who can then reproduce before they die." You get the idea! Indeed, if that *is* our ulti-mate purpose, then it all might seem rather pointless.

So, is there another way to answer the question 'Why do we exist?' or 'What is our purpose in life?'

I believe that there is. That's what this book is about.

You might expect me to say that my answer involves re-ligion and not science. Well, you'd be both right and wrong! That's because it's my view that understanding the answer involves *both* religion *and* science.

As indicated above, I've spent my professional life immersed in the science of biological molecules and cells—developing hypotheses, undertaking laboratory experiments, analysing the data generated as evidence to test the hypotheses. This cycle is then repeated in order, incrementally, to improve knowledge and understanding of the workings of the immune system.

At the same time, I have been a Christian for as long as I can remember. In the first instance, this was because I was brought up as a Christian—and I'm very grateful to my parents and others during my childhood and adolescence for their influence and guidance in this. My adherence to religion has varied throughout my life. However, I've always believed in God, and that God's true nature is shown to us in Jesus.

For some people and, in particular, for some scientists, this is incomprehensible. They might say, "How can a scientist who deals with solid, measurable, material evidence and data in the *natural* world, believe in an invisible and scientifically undetectable God? How can a scientist believe in the concept of 'spirits' or, indeed, in anything to do with religion—anything *supernatural?*"

Well, there are all sorts of answers to that question. You'll probably be relieved to know that this book doesn't attempt to address all of them! What *is* addressed, however, is what I think is the false distinction between what's arbitrarily defined as 'natural' and 'supernatural'.

We shall examine data indicating that we are more than the molecules, cells and tissues that constitute our physical bodies. This includes evidence that our conscious minds can function independently of our physical brains. In addition, each year many thousands of people provide personal testimony of experiencing a 'spiritual dimension' and meeting a 'higher spiritual power'. This occurs when they undergo what's known as 'Near-Death Experiences' (NDEs) during life-threatening events (such as severe heart attacks). Skeptical people argue that NDEs must be dreams or hallucinations triggered in a dying brain. But we'll examine the evidence that NDEs are real events, as is believed by the overwhelming majority of those who experience NDEs.

Further support for NDEs being 'real' (rather than imagined) events is the fact that many of the people who undergo NDEs experience lifelong, positive changes in their lives and their outlook on life is transformed. Indeed, they think that they have a much clearer understanding of the purpose of their lives.

In Part 1 of this book, we'll consider this evidence for a 'Spiritual Dimension' to reality. In Part 2, we'll then look at this evidence in the context of what many religious people have believed to be real for thousands of years.

So, let's launch into Chapter 1 by asking what you think is the purpose of *your* life.

Chapter 1

What's the point?

Why am I here?
Is there a point to it all?

What's the meaning of life?

These may, or may not, be questions you think about occasionally, if ever.

After all, there's plenty to be getting on with in life.

Depending on your age and situation, you may be concentrating on your education, aiming to be good at a sport, looking for a job, working hard at your career, looking for a life partner, raising a family, undertaking voluntary work, dealing with ill health, or simply coping with old age!

And then, in between all of these things, there's plenty to keep your mind occupied—radio, television, films, music, books, computer games, social media, keep-fit, playing sports, supporting your home team, socialising, DIY, gardening, vacations… you get the picture.

So, aren't all of these things that fill our lives enough to explain why we're here on planet Earth?

Well, maybe yes, maybe no.

In fact, is it a case of just getting through life—trying to be happy, trying to make others happy, and hoping not to do too much harm along the way?

And, at life's end—then what? Something or nothing? As each of us approaches death (and it's 100% certain that we will!)—do we view it as the 'beginning of the end' or the 'end of the beginning' of our existence?

Some years ago, I had a minor operation to remove varicose veins from my leg. It was the only time (so far!) that I've had a general anaesthetic. I remember lying on the trolley in the pre-op room while the initial sedative was administered. The surgeon came in to the room and I recall looking up at his smiling face and thinking "I don't feel at all drowsy—this anaesthetic isn't doing anything!"

And then, what seemed like a split second later, I found myself being awoken and, looking around, I realised I was in the post-op room! My right leg was swathed in bandages from thigh to foot; the surgical gown I was wearing had been cut apart, presumably so that the surgeons could get at the necessary bits of my body. Indeed, the latter caused me slight embarrassment because, as a lecturer in the Medical

Faculty, I realised that I would have taught some of the junior doctors and medical students who had been present at the operation!

But the dominant feeling that remained with me about that experience was that, while under the anaesthetic, I had no feelings at all—nothing, zilch. It wasn't like being asleep; it was more a feeling that my consciousness—my mind—had been totally annihilated for a period of time. And I remember thinking, "Is that what it's like to be dead?"

There are quite a lot of people who would say, "Yes, that's probably pretty much what death is like—you don't know anything about it because you no longer exist once you've died. Your 'being' has been obliterated."

Indeed, the neuroscientist Anil Seth, who's spent many years researching the neurological basis of consciousness, says exactly this about his own experience of general anaesthesia:

> Five years ago, for the third time in my life, I ceased to exist. I was having a small operation and my brain was filling with anaesthetic. I remember sensations of blackness, detachment, and falling apart…. Under general anaesthesia… I could have been under for five minutes, five hours, five years— or even fifty. And 'under' doesn't quite express it. I was simply not there, a premonition of the total oblivion of death.[1]

Some of the people, like Anil Seth, who would say this—and may have thought about these things a great deal—are what are known as 'materialists' (Seth actually prefers the term 'physicalist'). This is because they believe that there is nothing 'real' beyond the physical 'materials' (that's the matter and energy) which make up the universe in which we live. Thus, they argue, what we call our 'mind' or 'consciousness' isn't a real thing that exists in its own right: it's simply the result of the workings of our brain. So, therefore, when the brain dies, the mind disappears—it no longer exists. It would be rather like your computer crashing irretrievably (and you don't have it backed up!)—all your photos, music, e-mails, documents, etc. etc., are gone forever.

Materialists therefore conclude that there is no 'Afterlife' for us to experience once we die because they believe there is nothing after life! In other words, they believe that there is no 'Spiritual Dimension' to reality. Furthermore, many materialists also believe there is no God, because they say that there is no material evidence for God's existence, and there's no evidence for anything 'spiritual'. Thus, many materialists are also atheists.

The inevitable conclusion for a materialistic atheist is, therefore, that there is no ultimate purpose to our lives. They may well say, and strongly believe, that each of us should live the best life we can—aim to be happy, strive to help others, use our talents to achieve the best we can for ourselves, for humanity and the future of our planet. But, once we die, that's the end of everything for each of us. Furthermore, they believe that, because there is no God, there is nothing beyond ourselves that has any interest in what's best for us—there is no 'benevolence' or 'love' at the heart of reality.

This has been put bluntly and starkly by the widely known atheist, Richard Dawkins:

> In a universe of electrons and selfish genes, blind physical forces and genetic replication, some people are going to get hurt, other people are going to get lucky, and you won't find any rhyme or reason in it, nor any justice. The universe that we observe has precisely the properties we should expect if there is, at bottom, no design, no purpose, no evil, no good, nothing but pitiless indifference.[2]

Things To Think About
FOR REFLECTION AND DISCUSSION

1) What are your top five priorities in life?
2) What do you most look forward to each day; each week; in life?
3) Do you ever think about the meaning of life?

4) Do you think there is anything other than the
    'physical world'? Anything 'spiritual'?

5) Do you ever think about what happens after death?
    What do you think is most likely?

6) If life has no ultimate purpose, does this bother you,
    or affect how you live your life?

Chapter 2

Seeing is believing

Richard Dawkins, who I quoted at the end of the previous chapter, is a scientist—more specifically, he's an evolutionary biologist. Many scientists have materialist and atheist views about the nature of reality. However, other scientists believe that there *is* a Spiritual Dimension to reality, that God exists, and that there is an Afterlife: in other words, death isn't the end.

So, being a scientist doesn't mean having to be an atheist.

Conversely, there are many atheists in the world who are *not* scientists. Interestingly, this is particularly the case in so-called 'modernised' countries, such as in Europe, North America and Australasia.

The gradual loss of religious belief across the population—what's known as 'secularisation'—has been progressing in these countries for at least the last 150 years.[3] There are probably many different reasons for this, including increased education and individuality (so you don't feel the need to believe what religious leaders tell you to believe!); improved living conditions and life expectancy (so death isn't always 'just around the corner!'); and the vastly increased range of 'other things to do' that occupy people's minds and time (listed in Chapter 1), causing religion to be side-lined or deemed to be of no importance.

However, it isn't just that people are so occupied with other things that they don't feel they have time to think about God; it's also that increasing numbers of people state that they simply don't believe in God—they are atheists.

And this brings us back to materialism.

First, it's thanks to the tremendous success of the material sciences (physics, chemistry, biology, and so on) over the past 400 years or so that we now live in a world where technical and medical advances have made us feel that we're 'masters of our own destiny.' So where's the need for God?

Secondly—and I would say even more importantly— the understanding of the material world and the ordering of nature that science has made possible, has had a wide-ranging 'secularising' effect on how people view existence and reality. The materialist view has infiltrated all areas of life—education, the arts, politics, radio and television and everyday social interactions including, these days, all forms of social media. Although some people are not strongly opposed to religion (although others are!), many regard being religious as just a rather quirky (and pointless) life-style choice.

But what if, in fact, the religiously disinterested majority are wrong? What if there really is a 'Spiritual Dimension', there is a God, there is an Afterlife?

Well, they may say, "Where's the evidence?"

Indeed, when the philosopher Bertrand Russell was asked how he would justify his atheism if he found himself before God when he died, Russell replied "Not enough evidence, God, not enough evidence!"

Things To Think About

FOR REFLECTION AND DISCUSSION

---

1) What do you think are the three main reasons why many people don't believe in God?

2) Do you think it's likely that the decline in religious belief in many 'modernised' countries will continue, or might it be reversed?

3) What influences in society do you think have the greatest effect on whether or not people believe in God?

4) Do you think Bertrand Russell made a valid point when he said that there's not enough evidence to believe in God?

Chapter 3

Apologise, without saying sorry

So what evidence do religious believers, and Christians in particular, give to justify their faith?

Well, there are numerous lines of argument—these are what theologians call 'Apologetics.'[4] It's fair to say, however, that most of these arguments are consistent with the existence of God rather than providing direct evidence for the existence of God.

Here are just some examples, and possible counter-arguments that materialists and skeptics might raise:

Some people are convinced they have personal, first-hand experience of God's presence and love. This may be described as a 'conversion event' or 'a moment of transcendence'. For example, John Wesley, who founded the Methodist Church, spoke of a particular moment during a church service when he felt his 'heart strangely warmed': he already believed in God, but this was the instant at which he felt completely convinced of God's real presence with him.

> *Counter-argument:* Materialists would suggest that such experiences are entirely psychological—generated by the brain of the 'believer'—what might be called a type of 'wishful thinking' and self-induced euphoria.

Miracles happen that don't have a scientific explanation. Let's consider someone with terminal cancer—the doctors have given them a few weeks to live. Their religious friends and relatives pray earnestly for a miraculous healing. The patient goes for a medical check-up and, lo and behold, the cancer has unexpectedly regressed rather than grown; within a few weeks it has gone completely. The doctors are flummoxed; everyone is overjoyed by this miracle.

> *Counter-argument:* Skeptics may say that, however welcome and marvellous this recovery is, it's not miraculous: there's still a lot we don't know about disease processes and how the body can mend itself, and that sometimes this happens spontaneously in

ways we don't yet understand. Indeed, because of what we do now understand about biology and disease processes, and the advances in medical therapies that this has made possible, some current successful medical treatments would seem miraculous to our ancestors.

The human sense of morals must derive from a 'higher source'. I remember watching a nature programme about lions. One 'upstart' male, who'd reached full maturity and prowess, decided to try his luck against the dominant male, resulting in an almighty scrap. The dominant male lost—he was deposed. The young pretender took over the role of top dog (well, actually top lion, of course). He asserted himself over the lionesses of the Pride and, most shockingly, proceeded to kill all the cubs that had been fathered by his defeated opponent! Not very pleasant but, "Hey, that's nature, red in tooth and claw", you might say, "survival of the fittest." However, if the same happened in a human context, there would be, literally, moral outrage. If a man competed for, and secured the affections of, a woman at the expense of her previous partner, well it happens (quite often!). But, if he then killed the woman's children because he wasn't their father, that would be seen by all humanity as an inexcusable act of evil. So why is it OK for other animals to exhibit such massively selfish and callous behaviour at the expense of other members of their own species, but not us? This is the so-called 'Moral Argument'—that we humans are imbued with a higher moral sense that transcends mere instinct for survival and has been given to us by a 'higher moral agency', i.e. God.

> *Counter-argument:* Some would counter by saying, "Don't under-estimate evolution!" The more advanced organisms become, and therefore the more intricate the societies they develop, then the more complex must be the evolutionary processes that have generated these organisms and their societies. So, human morality may be just an advanced form of evolutionary adaptation in which the good of society has out-competed the good of the individual.

The universe had a beginning, so it must have had a Creator. A hundred years ago most scientists believed the universe to be eternal—it had always existed and always would exist. They had no solid evidence for this—it just seemed to make the most sense scientifically. However, evidence gradually accumulated indicating that the universe did have a beginning—there was a time when the universe didn't exist, but then it sprang into being. This creation event happened 13.8 billion years ago (or there abouts), and is now famously known as the The Big Bang. Some scientists were unhappy with this theory, not because it wasn't consistent with the data, but because it raised the possibility of a Creator of the universe, i.e. God, which scientists who were materialistic atheists found unpalatable. So, it may not be very similar to the Book of Genesis, but a creator God fits with the physics!

> *Counter-argument:* Some physicists argue that, according to quantum theory, there doesn't have to have been a First Cause that brought the universe into being—it could have happened for no reason!

Creation is incredibly 'fine-tuned' for our existence. Physicist have found that just slight changes in any of several key parameters that determine the nature of the universe (e.g. the strength of gravity) would so alter the structure of the universe that it couldn't support any sort of life, including us. Indeed, the likelihood of a universe like ours arising purely by chance is almost infinitesimally small. This therefore suggests that the universe was 'designed' to support life, so it must have had a designer, i.e. God.

> *Counter-argument:* According to the Multiverse Hypothesis, there may actually be a very large number of universes—perhaps an infinite number. Even if only one of these has exactly the right properties to support life like us, that's obviously the universe

in which we will find ourselves existing, and it's the only universe that we can know.

The requirements for life to exist are too complex for it to have happened spontaneously. The 'origin of species' is one thing (that we won't consider right now!)—but what about the initial origin of life itself? How did the Earth go from being a place with nothing living on it, to a place where life is present? Well, basically, nobody knows. Scientists have generated hypotheses and performed experiments for decades, but nobody has any clear ideas as to how matters could progress from a few of the chemical building blocks of life to a functioning, feeding, self-reproducing, living thing without it having been designed and created. So perhaps it was designed and created—by God.

> *Counter-argument:* Just because scientists are scratching their heads about the spontaneous origin of life now, doesn't mean that it will always be like that. Scientific advance has involved numerous breakthroughs in understanding that had previously been inconceivable, so the same may be true for origins of life research.

The examples given above are just a few of the ways in which arguments can be made for the existence of God.

However, as is clear in each case, it's quite possible to formulate counter arguments as to why other explanations are feasible that don't require God to exist! This is at least partly because the lines of evidence are indirect—as stated earlier, the evidence is consistent with the existence of God, but doesn't *prove* the existence of God.

So is it possible to do better than this? Well, let's give it a go!

Things To Think About

FOR REFLECTION AND DISCUSSION

---

1) Do you ever have a sense of something 'other' than the physical world around us?

2) Do you believe that miracles happen? Why? Or why not?

3) Why do we have morals?

4) Do scientific concepts have any bearing on religion?

5) Rate how convincing you find each of the six arguments in this Chapter as evidence for the existence of God.

Chapter 4

It's a paradox!

We'll start by returning to the materialist assumption, mentioned in Chapter 1, that the mind is simply the result of the workings of our brain—when the brain dies, the mind disappears.

From the materialist's perspective, this is the only point of view that makes sense, and so it's presented as though it's a proven, undeniable fact. Indeed, this is exactly how the neuroscientist Anil Seth puts it—again referring to his experience of general anaesthesia highlighted in Chapter 1: "Our conscious experiences are part of nature just as our bodies are, just as our world is. And when life ends, consciousness will end too. When I think about this, I am transported back to my experience—my non-experience—of anaesthesia. To its oblivion, perhaps comforting, but oblivion nonetheless."[1]

Note Seth's bold statement: "When life ends, consciousness will end too." Nowhere in this statement does he use the words 'may', 'possibly' or 'perhaps'! But, as I've already said, this is just one scientific point of view, not a proven fact.

Indeed, the psychologist Robert Epstein presents a very different scientific point of view in an article entitled, "Brain as Transducer: What if the brain is not a self-contained information processor? What if it is simply a transducer?"[5] In essence, Epstein proposes that the mind is not generated by the brain, but is a separate entity. What this means is that the brain doesn't *produce* the mind, but rather that the brain *channels* the mind from elsewhere into our world of physical matter and energy.

The analogy Epstein uses for the brain acting as a transducer of the mind is when we hear someone's voice coming out of a radio, phone or earpiece—these 'bits of kit' are obviously not generating the voice, but are *transducing* the electrical signals they receive to be heard as a voice that we recognise and understand.

So where might the mind come from if it's not produced by the brain? Well, Epstein points out that theories of modern physics predict the existence of other universes to ours. Some of these theories also predict that reality is composed of as many as eleven dimensions: so, after subtracting the four dimensions that our senses detect, this still leaves plenty of other dimensions where our mind might come from!

The thought that the mind and the body are separate things isn't new—it goes back to the French philosopher Rene Descartes in the seventeenth century, and even further back to Plato in Ancient Greece. Indeed, we might say that Epstein is proposing, on scientific grounds, that we have a soul! I am confident, however, that he wouldn't be comfortable with this interpretation given its religious connotations; indeed, he states that "the main reason we should give serious thought to such a [transduction] theory has nothing to do with ghosts. It has to do with the sorry state of brain science and its pathetic reliance on the computer metaphor."[5]

So, as a pragmatic scientist, what evidence does Epstein call upon to support the mind/brain transduction theory? One of the key lines of evidence he cites is something called 'Paradoxical Lucidity' (or 'Terminal Lucidity'). This refers to situations where patients with advanced dementia (or other causes of severely compromised brain function), close to the time of death, become remarkably and inexplicably mentally lucid—for example, being able to hold conversations and recall names and events far better than they have for a long time previously.[6] So, at a time when their brain function should be the most severely reduced, their mind seems to clear of the brain fog; and this is apparent to all of those around them—relatives and medical staff alike. This last point is important for treating paradoxical lucidity as evidence of mind/brain separation because it involves independent observers (i.e. people other than the person who is actually experiencing the phenomenon) witnessing the event and verifying that it actually occurred.

Numerous cases of paradoxical lucidity have been reported in the medical literature over the past 250 years. A relatively recent case recounted by Michael Nahm and his colleagues concerned an elderly Icelandic woman with Alzheimer's disease. She was living in a care home where she was visited regularly by members of her family, although she had not recognised or spoken to them for a year. However, on one occasion a few weeks before she died, she sat up and spoke to her son Lydur, who was visiting her at the time. "My Lydur", she said, "I am going to recite a verse to you." She then recited a verse from a psalm written by an Icelandic poet before lying back and becoming unresponsive again.[6]

And here's a different type of disease example in a young man in whom cancer cells had largely destroyed and replaced his brain tissue: "In the days before his death, he lost all ability to speak or move. According to a nurse and his wife, however, an hour before he died, he woke up and said goodbye to his family, speaking with them for about five minutes before losing consciousness again and dying."[7]

These are not just highly unusual, isolated occurrences: well-organised, systematic research is finding many examples of paradoxical lucidity that cannot be shrugged off and ignored.

So what's the materialist explanation for paradoxical lucidity? Well, as far as I'm aware, there isn't one that's convincing. In any situation where a person's brain is so damaged and degenerated that the normal functions of the mind (such as recognition, recall and communication) are missing, it seems impossible that these functions should return spontaneously and suddenly if they have to be *generated* by the brain.

By contrast, if the mind exists in its own right—apart from the brain—then paradoxical lucidity can be explained by the mind, at least for a short time, freeing itself from the constraints of the degenerating brain as death approaches. This may allow the conscious mind to express itself once again via the sub-conscious (which is, presumably, still functional) before it finally separates entirely from the body at the point of death.

Thus, if the brain is, indeed, a transducer (rather than generator) of the mind, then the death of the brain shouldn't destroy the mind—rather, it should *free* the mind from the constraints that the brain places on it during life.

Things To Think About

FOR REFLECTION AND DISCUSSION

1) Do you think that if a scientist states something about the topic in which that scientist is an expert, then it must be true?

2) Where do you think your mind comes from?

3) Have you ever heard of 'Paradoxical Lucidity' ('Terminal Lucidity') before?

4) Have you ever witnessed anything like 'Paradoxical Lucidity'? Or do you know anyone else who has?

5) Can you think of a reasonable explanation for Paradoxical Lucidity other than it being due to the mind being 'released' from the constraints of a degenerating brain?

Chapter 5

Out-of-body, but not out of mind!

So, if the mind continues to exist and function when the body dies, where does it go?

Well, the evidence indicates that, in some cases, the answer to that question is not very far at all—at least in the first instance.

"Hang on", you might say. "What do you mean again by 'evidence'? Evidence has to be something that can be validated independently."

I agree—that's a fair point, which brings us to out-of-body experiences.

Out-of-Body Experiences (OBEs) are usually (but not exclusively) a part of what are called Near-Death Experiences (NDEs). We'll consider the general features of NDEs more fully in subsequent chapters, but a broad definition of NDEs is that they are vivid, memorable, highly meaningful and transformative spiritual experiences that occur during an episode when a person comes close to death, but with subsequent recovery.

Although accounts of NDEs have arisen across the world and throughout history, the term 'Near-Death Experience' was introduced only in 1975 by Dr Raymond Moody, a psychiatrist who undertook one of the first detailed investigations of a large number of NDEs and reported his findings in his book *Life After Life*.[8] This helped to trigger a wider interest in NDEs amongst clinicians and scientists, leading to a plethora of research studies and publications (including research papers in high profile medical and scientific journals).

Thousands of NDEs have been reported and studied over the last 40-50 years. In fact, NDEs are surprisingly common—over 4% (1 in 25) of the population have had some sort of NDE. These can vary greatly in the precise nature and intensity (or 'depth') of the experience, as will be discussed in the next chapter.

Out-of-body experiences occur in about three-quarters of people who undergo NDEs (we'll call them 'NDErs' or just the 'subjects'). The OBE refers to the experience of the subject's 'mind' or 'consciousness' separating from their physical body and viewing their body and events around it from an external location. Given that NDEs frequently occur while the subject is in a hospital emergency room (e.g. following a heart attack), or in an operating theatre, the OBE may involve them reporting that they floated away from their body and near to the ceiling of the room from where they viewed their body lying on the bed or trolley and the medical staff working (sometimes frantically!) around their body. This is why I said earlier that the mind may not travel very far from the body when it first separates from it!

The value of the OBE as a source of evidence for the reality of mind/brain separation is that, in many cases, the events the patient claims to have witnessed while unconscious and close to death match the medical staff's recollection of events. For example, a particularly remarkable example was described in a study of NDEs published in the highly reputable medical journal *The Lancet*:

A nurse described helping with a man brought in to hospital who had suffered a heart attack and was in a coma. In order to insert a tube into his throat, the nurse removed the patient's false teeth and put them onto a trolley. Once the patient was stable, but still unconscious, the nurse left the room and didn't see the patient again until a week later, when he was recovering on the cardiac ward. As soon as he saw the nurse, the patient said, "Oh, that nurse knows where my dentures are." Not surprisingly, the nurse was very surprised, but the patient went on to describe how he'd seen himself lying in bed and watched this nurse remove his teeth and put them on the trolley. He also accurately described the room in which he was resuscitated and the other medical staff present at the time.[9]

This is just one example of many, reported by numerous researchers and clinicians. For example, from his studies on OBEs and NDEs in the 1970s mentioned above, Raymond Moody stated that "[s]everal doctors have told me…that they are utterly baffled about how patients with no medical knowledge could describe in such detail and so correctly the procedure used in resuscitation attempts, even though these events took place while the doctors knew the patients involved to be 'dead'."[8]

When the cardiologist Michael Sabom heard Raymond Moody speak about his study of NDEs and was asked what he thought about it, Sabom said, "I don't believe it!" This led him to start asking his own patients if they'd experienced NDEs and was shocked to find that some had! Sabom then undertook his own detailed investigation in which he showed that patients' accounts of what they 'saw' during their OBEs (while unconscious) were remarkably consistent with events as recorded in their medical records, and as recounted by other people present at the time.[10] With regard to the OBE recounted by one patient, Sabom said, "When I asked him to tell me what exactly he saw, he described the resuscitation with such detail and accuracy that I could have later used the tape to teach physicians."[11]

By contrast, Sabom found that nearly all patients who did not experience OBEs made major errors when asked to guess what had happened during their medical procedures.

Penny Sartori is another researcher who also reported from her studies that "...this research has demonstrated that those who reported OBEs gave more accurate descriptions of events and equipment used than those who were resuscitated, but did not report a NDE/OBE. This lends... support to the possibility of consciousness existing apart from the brain."[12]

A particularly relevant personal recollection of his OBE (and NDE) was recounted by Dr Rajiv Parti. He was a senior anaesthesiologist who underwent surgery for a serious, drug-resistant abdominal infection. During the surgery, Rajiv left his body and watched the operation from above while also hearing the conversation between the members of the surgical team. At one point, the anaesthesiologist who had sedated Rajiv, told a rather risqué joke that made the rest of the surgical team laugh. When the anaesthesiologist came to visit Rajiv after the operation, Rajiv told him about the OBE and the joke he'd told. The anaesthesiologist replied, "Oh really? And what was the joke?" Rajiv goes on the say, "I recalled it for him, the ribald joke that made the surgeon and operating room staff laugh. The anaesthesiologist blushed when I told the joke. 'I must not have given you enough anaesthesia,' he said. 'No, you gave me plenty,' I replied, recounting the amount of medication I had seen him administer."[13]

We thus see that the phenomena of OBEs and paradoxical lucidity, provide evidence that can be verified by independent observers. These events cannot be explained by materialism, which assumes that the mind is generated by the brain so that when the physical brain ceases to function, the mind disappears. By contrast, OBEs and paradoxical lucidity *can* be explained if reality is more than the physical realm of materialism—if, in fact, there is what could be called a 'Spiritual Dimension' to reality in which the mind continues to exist after the brain has ceased to function. In this context, it might then be reasonable to refer to 'the mind' as 'the soul'.

Things To Think About
FOR REFLECTION AND DISCUSSION

---

1) Can you think of a good explanation for an OBE other than it being due to the mind separating from the body but continuing to function and generate consciousness?

2) Are you surprised that research studies in North America and Europe have found that as many as 4% of people (1 in 25) have experienced an NDE? What percentage would you have expected for this?

3) Have you ever experienced an OBE? Or do you know anyone else who has?

4) What further evidence would you like to see to convince you that OBEs are 'real' events rather than 'imagined'?

5) If you were a medical doctor, what would you say to a recovering patient who told you that they'd watched you while they were unconscious and could accurately recount in detail what you did to save them from dying?

Chapter 6

More than a dream

As mentioned in Chapter 5, an 'Out-of-Body Experience' is just one aspect of what's become known as the 'Near-Death Experience' and refers to what is perceived close to the body of the subject where independent observers (e.g. medical staff) may corroborate what the 'mind' of the subject claims to have seen.

However, in many cases, the OBE is just the first part of the overall experience and, for many who have these experiences, their OBE isn't the most significant part by a long stretch!

As a fairly typical example of an NDE, here's an account recorded by Bruce Greyson.[14] Greyson is a psychiatrist who spent over forty years researching NDEs. This account was given by Bill Herlund who, as a firefighter at an American Air Force Base in 1970, went to deal with a burning plane that exploded as he approached it—the blast slammed his body into the side of his truck, at which point he lost consciousness. He then witnessed two other fire fighters dragging away a body. He realised that this was his own body, but he "could see everything much more clearly and felt warm, safe, and peaceful." Then, a further explosion knocked over the other two fire fighters on top of his body. Bill then found himself in a tunnel "like the inside of a tornado" with a light in the distance that he was rapidly drawn towards. He realised that the source of the light was a beautiful 'Being' who also radiated unconditional love and peace. By thought-transfer, this 'Light Being' asked Bill how he felt about his life and how he had treated other people. Bill went on to say:

> As he asked, every single event of my life from earliest childhood to the plane crash projected in front of me. There were details concerning people and things that I had forgotten about long ago. I was not proud of some of my dealings with other people, but the light was quick to forgive all of my errors. He told me to 'be in peace' and said that my work in this world was not done yet, and that I had to go back, and I was gone. I was back in my body again.[14]

No two NDEs are completely identical, but they do contain some 'core elements' that are reported across many NDEs from around the world by people of different cultures, ethnicities, ages and religions (or of no religion).

In a 2011 study of 1,300 NDEs from around the world, the radiation oncologist Jeffrey Long identified common elements of NDEs (several of which were evident in Bill Herlund's NDE summarised above).[15] In addition to the out-of-body experience considered in Chapter 5, these common elements included:

- Heightened senses ('more conscious and alert than normal')
- Intense and generally positive emotions or feelings ('incredible peace')
- Passing into or through a tunnel
- Encountering a mystical or brilliant light
- Encountering other beings, either mystical beings or deceased relatives or friends
- Undergoing a Life Review (scenes from throughout life are replayed)
- Encountering unworldly ('heavenly') realms
- Being aware of a decision to return to their body

More recently, in 2022, a group of eighteen scientists and clinicians from twelve Universities and Medical Centres in the USA and UK published consensus guidelines for the definition and study of NDEs.[16] This group was led by Sam Parnia and included Jeffrey Long, as well as Bruce Greyson and Peter Fenwick who are also quoted in this book. The group proposed that 'authentic NDEs' should be renamed 'Recalled Experiences of Death' (REDs) and they defined six key stages or themes that are reported in the majority of NDEs/REDs and that incorporate the elements above identified by Long. The six stages are:

(1) Perceived death and separation from the body;
(2) Heading to a 'destination';
(3) Reliving the recording of Life—actions and intentions matter;
(4) A sense of being 'home';
(5) Returning back to life;
(6) After-effects of the experience.

This provides a clearly defined basis for the scientific study of NDEs/REDs going forward and the future directions of this research.[16]

Before considering some of these NDE features in more detail, it's again worth asking the question, "What's the evidence that these events are real, rather than being made up (i.e., imagined) by the desperate workings of a highly stressed, dying brain?"

Well, firstly, we've already seen in the previous chapter that many OBE accounts are independently corroborated by others present when the subject was close to death, e.g., medical staff and relatives. However, such eyewitness validation clearly isn't possible for the 'transcendent' aspects of NDEs such as travelling through a tunnel, meeting mystical beings and/or deceased relatives, undergoing a 'Life Review', and so on.

What researchers have therefore done is carefully scrutinize the common features of many NDEs to determine whether they are more consistent with reports of real events, or the nature of events experienced during hallucinations, dreams or other types of imagined events. For example, Jeffrey Long published a journal article that details nine lines of evidence indicating that NDEs are real, rather than imagined, experiences. In addition to the verification of OBEs discussed in Chapter 5, these lines of evidence include the following:[17]

- NDEs experienced by people of different nationalities and different racial, cultural and religious backgrounds are similar. This is consistent with the reality of NDEs, since imagined events associated with dreams or hallucinations might be expected to vary markedly based on the diversity of the individuals involved and the circumstances of their NDEs.

- NDEs reported by children under the age of 5 years are not significantly different from those reported by older children and adults. Young children are unlikely to have strongly established religious beliefs or understanding of death, so the similarities between their NDEs and those of older individuals suggest their experiences are real rather than imagined events based on cultural expectations.

- NDEs are lucid, organized experiences as distinct from muddled or vague experiences as might be associated with hallucinations, delirium or dreams. Indeed, the majority report that during their NDEs they feel "more conscious and alert than normal". Long reported that, in a survey of 1,122 NDEs, 95.6% of those surveyed said that their NDE was 'definitely real' and 4.0% that their NDE was 'probably real'; thus only 0.4% (i.e., 4 people) thought that their NDE was not real.[17]

- NDEs including 'seeing events and people' have been reported by blind people, including some blind from birth.[18,19] In fact, Robert Epstein presents this as another line of evidence (in addition to 'Paradoxical Lucidity' discussed in Chapter 4) in support of the 'Brain as Transducer' concept.[5] In some cases, it's been possible to verify from independent witnesses with normal vision that what blind subjects say that they 'saw' during their OBEs was correct.

Here's the example of Brad Barrows, who was blind from birth, reported by Kenneth Ring and Sharon Cooper.[18] When Brad was 8 years old, he experienced an OBE/NDE during an episode of severe pneumonia; he found himself unable to breathe and was later told by nurses that his heart stopped beating for four minutes. Brad felt himself float up from his bed towards the ceiling. From there he could see his own body still on the bed. He witnessed his roommate leave the room to get help. Brad then passed up through the roof and above the building. From there he surveyed the surrounding streets (that were covered in snow and slush) and recognised a nearby playground and hill that he used to visit. Brad then "…found himself in a tunnel and emerged from it to find himself in an immense field illuminated by a tremendous, all-encompassing light…. He found himself walking on a path surrounded by tall grass, and also re-ported seeing tall trees with immense leaves…. Brad en-countered a man whom he didn't recognize but from whom emanated an overwhelming love. The man, without a word, gently nudged Brad backward, initiating a reversal of his experience, ending with his finding himself in bed gasping for air, attended by two nurses."[18]

Through all of this experience, Brad was amazed that he could actually 'see'!

If the brain alone is responsible for the sensation of sight, then experiences such as Brad's are inexplicable. If, however, the mind (or soul) is the ultimate source of 'being', Brad's experience can be explained by the mind being freed from the constraints of a defective brain, as we also discussed as an explanation for Paradoxical Lucidity.

Not surprisingly, many hypotheses have been proposed to try to explain OBEs and NDEs from a materialist point of view—that is, based solely on changes in brain function rather than the mind separating from the body, which implies the existence of a 'spiritual reality'. Several books provide detailed consideration of the main materialist explanations for OBEs and NDEs, but conclude that none satisfactorily explain the range of features of these phenomena[20-23].

In his journal article mentioned above, Jeffrey Long concludes that:

> …there have been over 20 different "explanations" of NDE suggested that cover the gamut of physiological, psychological, and cultural causes. If anyone or several of these "explanations" were widely accepted as plausible, then there would be no need for so many different "explanations" of NDE. Among

those who believe that physical brain function must explain everything that is experienced in all NDEs, there is no consensus whatsoever about how physical brain function produces NDEs.... The combination of the... lines of evidence converges on the conclusion that near-death experiences are medically inexplicable... [and provide] powerful evidence that NDEs are, in a word, real.[17]

Things To Think About

FOR REFLECTION AND DISCUSSION

---

1) When the doctor told Bill Herlund that he had 'nearly died' during the incident with the burning plane, Bill replied, 'I did die'. The doctor looked at Bill quizzically and then referred him for psychiatric assessment![14] How do you think that made Bill feel?

2) Out of the common elements of NDEs identified in Jeffrey Long's study, which do you find most difficult to believe (if not all of them!)?

3) Four arguments are listed in this Chapter to support the reality of NDEs. These are: similarity between NDEs across all cultures; similarity between NDEs in children and adults; most NDErs believe them to be real; blind subjects have 'sight' during their

NDEs. Which of these arguments do you find most convincing? Which do you find least convincing?

4) If you had to think up a 'materialist' explanation for NDEs, what would you propose as the most likely cause of NDEs? Could this explanation account for all the features of NDEs discussed in this chapter?

Chapter 7

Opposite poles: positive and negative NDEs

The majority of NDErs report encountering other 'spiritual beings' during their transcendent experiences. This includes meeting deceased relatives and friends—indeed, this sometimes includes seeing people the NDEr was not aware had already died! These are recounted as being joyous reunions.

There are also numerous accounts of being met by 'angelic beings'. However, the most frequently reported encounter, that also leaves the greatest impression on the NDEr, is with a supreme or divine 'Being of Light'.

A typical account was given in Chapter 6 in the description by the fire fighter Bill Herlund of his NDE: "The light was emanating from a being that was giving off a very brilliant light as part of his essence. He was beautiful to look at, and projected the feelings of unconditional love and peace."[14]

In this case, Bill doesn't ascribe a specific name to this 'Being of Light'. In fact, this type of encounter is reported by NDErs across all cultures and religions and, indeed, by those who do not espouse any religion. For example, Bruce Greyson recounts how Suzanne Ingram, who regarded herself as a lapsed Catholic, underwent an NDE following a car accident and described her experience as follows: "I recall meeting my Creator. Call this Creator what you will: God, Buddha, Krishna, Allah. It does not matter. I will call him God for simplifying this, but do not refer to any particular religion or God."[14]

By contrast, it's usual for NDErs of a particular religious faith immediately to recognise the 'Being of Light' in the context of their religious beliefs. For example, a young Christian Middle Eastern woman called Samaa Habib was caught in the blast of a terrorist's bomb in the church she was attending.[24] The explosion threw her against a wall. She instantly lost consciousness and found herself face-to face with Jesus: "His face was brighter than the sun, and He was so glorious…He radiated an amazing love that contained deep acceptance. "Welcome home, Samaa," he said in a voice sweet and gentle, yet also powerful, like the sound of many waters. He opened His arms to me… Like a magnet, His love drew me in."[24]

The 'personal' nature of this encounter is especially striking: "Welcome home, Samaa." said Jesus.[24] I certainly have the impression that some of the most vivid and specific NDEs are those with a 'Christian' foundation. In some Christian-based accounts the NDEr claims to have met God (rather than Jesus), or both God *and* Jesus.

The over-arching impression, however, is that the 'Being of Light' radiates absolute, unconditional love and acceptance.

As a caveat to what's been described above, it has to be said that not all NDEs can be described as 'pleasant', 'positive' or 'heavenly'. About 15-20% of reported NDEs would be better described as 'distressing', 'negative' or 'hellish'! A number of books provide detailed consideration of such NDEs[14, 21, 26, 27].

At least some of these distressing experiences may not be true NDEs, but may actually be nightmarish hallucinations induced by anaesthetics or recreational drugs[26]—what might be called 'bad trips'!

In other cases, however, the distressing experience could be interpreted as a state of 'separation from God' that, in numerous cases, is turned around by appealing *to* God. An example of this is provided by the account of Ian McCormack, a scuba diver from New Zealand who was stung by five box jellyfish and died in the hospital for 15-20 minutes.[28] Ian found himself in a place of utter darkness and bitter cold with a pervading sense of evil. Although it was too dark for him to see anything, he became aware of others around him who shouted at him that he was in hell. In the ambulance on the way to hospital, he'd asked God to forgive him for the way he'd lived his life, and he now cried out for God's help. Ian described what happened next:

> Then a brilliant light shone upon me and literally drew me out of the darkness. A voice spoke to me from the centre of the light: 'Ian, you must see in a new light.' I remembered being given a Christmas card, which said, 'Jesus is the light of the world,' and 'God is light and there is no darkness in him.' So this was God! To my amazement a wave of pure unconditional love flowed over me. Instead of judgment I was being washed with pure love. Pure, unadulterated, clean, uninhibited, undeserved, love. It began to fill me up from the inside out. This love was healing my heart and I began to understand that there is incredible hope for humankind in this love.[28]

It would be far too simplistic to conclude that 'good people' experience only 'positive NDEs' and 'bad people' experience only 'negative NDEs'—at least in terms of conventional human definitions of what constitutes being a 'good' or 'bad' person.

Not surprisingly, many who have undergone distressing NDEs struggle to come to terms with their experiences. Some of those who are most successful in doing so are those "who interpret their NDE as a warning, who are able to connect it with previous behaviours they identify as unwise or downright wrong, and who then find avenues by which to modify their lives in satisfying ways."[26]

A particularly striking example is provided by Howard Storm who was an atheist and successful university Professor of Art. He underwent a highly distressing NDE from which, similar to Ian McCormack, he was 'rescued' by appealing to Jesus. He subsequently gave up his academic career and became a Christian clergyman.[29] Indeed, following his NDE, Ian McCormack also went on to be ordained as a clergyman![28]

A further relevant example is provided by Dr Rajiv Parti who, as already mentioned in chapter 5, underwent an OBE, and also a particularly deep and vivid NDE while undergoing surgery[13]. Rajiv knew that he'd been living a highly selfish and materialistic life with little concern for the needs and feelings of others, including his own family. During his NDE he found himself, as he described it, "on the lip of hell."[13] He prayed for God to give him another chance, at which point he was met by the spirit of his deceased father, who led him away from his distressing predicament. Although Rajiv was a Hindu, he went on to meet what he recognised as two 'Christian Angels' who guided him to meet the Being of Light. Although he couldn't give a specific identity to this Being, in a subsequent transcendent encounter, the Being appeared to him as Jesus.[13]

Once he'd recovered from his surgery, Rajiv resigned his position as an anaesthesiologist and has devoted his life to the "consciousness-based healing" of people with addictions and/or depression.[13]

If one is prepared to entertain the idea that this 'Being of Light' represents the ultimate, Deity, Creator, God, Divine, First Cause or whatever other term one prefers, it seems reasonable to assume that we humans, with our limited capacities of intellect and imagination, can grasp no more than a tiny fraction of the true and full nature of such a Being. However, God (let's stick with that name!) knows and understands this immeasurably better than we can, and therefore goes well beyond 'halfway' to meet us at a point that we can cope with in the context of each culture's and person's religion and tradition. In this regard, it's my view that Christianity provides one of the best, or perhaps *the* best, meeting point between God and humanity, as evidenced by NDEs. In addition, this discussion may also help to explain how different NDErs can have somewhat differing encounters with the 'Being of Light' depending on their cultural and religious background, although this is actually one and the same 'Being'.

This is consistent with the views of Rajiv Parti who, although a Hindu, underwent a partly 'Christian' NDE, as described above. He says he "settled on the idea that people of all cultures have similar mystical experiences guiding them down the path of spiritual discovery."[13] And that he "made a decision to serve all religions, from Christian to Hindu and all others. [He] felt there was a consciousness common to them all, one that [he has] come to call 'universal consciousness'."[13]

Things To Think About

FOR REFLECTION AND DISCUSSION

---

1) If you had an NDE, which deceased relatives or friends would you most like to meet?
2) Do you believe that there are angels?
3) Why do you think that people of different cultures or religious beliefs (or of no religion) ascribe different identities to the 'Being of Light' that they claim to have encountered during their NDEs?
4) If you met the 'Being of Light', what identity (if any) would you ascribe to this being?

5) What do you think is the significance of the fact that many NDErs claim that the 'Being of Light' radiates 'unconditional love'?

6) Do you believe there is 'Heaven'? Do you believe there is 'Hell'?

7) How would you make sense of the NDE recounted by the scuba diver Ian McCormack?

8) Do you think there is ever a situation where 'all is irretrievably lost'?

9) Do you agree with Rajiv Parti that essentially all major religions point towards the same fundamental reality or, as he put it, 'universal consciousness'[13]?

Chapter 8

My whole life flashed before me!

"My life flashed before my eyes" is a well-known phrase often used in the context of someone having a 'brush with death.' As mentioned in previous chapters, this actually happens during a significant proportion of NDEs. It's usually called the 'Life Review'.

Bill Herlund described a life review that occurred during his NDE, recounted in Chapter 6. It's particularly pertinent that, in relation to this, the 'Being of Light' asked Bill: "How do you feel about your life?" and "How did you treat other people?"[14]

This, in fact, consistently seems to be the purpose of the Life Review—not so much to remind the NDEr what they'd done during their life, but to show how they treated other people! Indeed, in many cases, NDErs report that during their Life Review, not only did they witness the things they did and said to others, but also experienced what these others felt in response to their actions and words. Here's an example of a Life Review experienced by Rene Hope Turner and recounted by John Burke.[27] During her NDE, Rene found herself before a man who welcomed her:

> …with great Love, Tranquility, Peace…He stood beside me and directed me to look to my left, where I was replaying my life's less complimentary moments; I relived those moments and felt not only what I had done but also the hurt I had caused. Some of the things I would have never imagined could have caused pain. I was surprised that some things I may have worried about, like shoplifting a chocolate as a child, were not there while casual remarks which caused hurt unknown to me at the time were counted. When I became burdened with guilt, I was directed to other events which gave joy to others. Though I felt unworthy, it seemed the balance was in my favour. I received great Love.[27]

Indeed, the whole message of the Life Review seems to be to see how the NDEr measures up to the famous 'Golden Rule' that's central to most religions: 'Treat others as you want to be treated' or, as it's phrased in the Christian Gospels, *"Love your neighbour as yourself."*

Howard Storm, the atheist academic turned clergyman, briefly mentioned in the previous chapter, recounted part of the conversation he had with Jesus during his NDE as follows:

> [Jesus] said, "…Your purpose is to love the person that you're with." …And I said, "That's it?!…" And he said, "That's your whole purpose." And I said, "What good will that do?" And he said, "It will change the whole world…If you love the person that you're with, they'll love the person that they're with and they'll love the person that they're with. And that will multiply… Whether you believe it or not, whether you like it or not, it's God's plan. It will work. Just love the person that you're with."[25]

Whatever one's view is of the nature and meaning of NDEs, it's undeniable that many NDErs are permanently changed in their values, outlook on life and attitude towards death. In fact, in several ways, the changes seen in NDErs are similar to those often associated with a 'religious conversion'. This has been shown in numerous studies of NDEs. Furthermore, these 'life changes' are usually permanent, not just transitory. Common changes identified in those who have undergone NDEs, as summarised by Penny Sartori, include:[22]

- No longer having a fear of death. Because many NDErs are convinced by their experience that there is life after death and of the reality of Heaven, they no longer fear death as being 'the end of everything'.
- More loving and considerate to others. Many NDErs are convinced that our purpose on Earth is to love each other—as exemplified by the 'Being of Light' and highlighted in their Life Review.
- Less materialistic and status-seeking. The pursuit of wealth and the accumulation of material possessions becomes significantly less important to many NDErs. Similarly, striving for 'status' loses its appeal. This equates precisely with the message that 'worldly' values are not God's values.
- Enhanced appreciation of life. Although many NDErs admit that they didn't want to leave Heaven and return to Earth, they often show enhanced appreciation of the value of living, in the knowledge of how life on Earth relates to the Afterlife and the fulfilment of God's purposes.
- Change in spiritual values. For some NDErs, their experience leads to profound changes in their

spiritual values and/or religious commitment. This is exemplified in the lives of Ian McCormack[28] and Howard Storm[29], referred to previously.

- Sense of mission or purpose in life. Some NDErs feel that their recovery and return to life is intended to give them a 'second chance' to live out the values they learned during their NDE, and to use their experience to help others come to faith in God.

Things To Think About

FOR REFLECTION AND DISCUSSION

---

1) Thinking back over your life, if you underwent a 'Life Review', what would you expect to see in it?

2) Do you think it's just coincidence that most major religions around the world espouse the 'Golden Rule' (i.e. 'treat others as you want to be treated')?

3) How easy or difficult do you find it to love other people, regardless of who they are?

4) Do you fear dying? If so, why (or why not)?

5) What does 'love' mean to you? How important is it?

6) Put the following in order of importance to you: money, material possessions, status, success, happiness, relationships, justice, doing the right thing, helping others.

7) Do you have a 'sense of purpose' in your life?

8) If a close friend or relative of yours experienced
    an NDE that radically changed their values and
    priorities in life, how would you respond to this?
    Might it affect your relationship with them?

Chapter 9

So what *is* the point of it all?

So, based on the phenomena of Paradoxical Lucidity, OBEs and NDEs, I propose that the conclusions that are most consistent with all of this evidence are that:

- Materialism describes only a part of reality;
- The brain is a transducer, not producer, of the mind[5];
- A 'Spiritual Dimension' is a part of reality;
- We have a 'soul' (another name for the 'mind' as separate from the 'body');
- There is 'life after death' (rather than 'nothing');
- God exists (recognised by some NDErs as the 'Being of Light').

Which brings us back to where we started: 'Why are you here?' or 'What's the point of it all'

Well, the point of it all then seems quite straight forward—we're here to learn what God wants us to do, which is 'to love each other'.

This is how Crystal McVea put it—she'd had a difficult life as a child and teenager but, as an adult, underwent an NDE during an acute episode of pancreatitis:

> …standing in [God's] glorious presence, filled with His infinite wisdom, there was still one question I felt compelled to ask… 'Why? Why didn't I do more for You?…Why didn't I do what You asked me to do?' It's not that I felt regret—it's that I loved God so immensely I felt like He deserved so much more from me. But God wouldn't allow me to feel bad about it. There is no feeling bad in heaven…. He is a loving God. I realized I didn't just love God. I realized He IS love.[30]

And, even more so—accepting that our 'material' life here on Earth is just the prelude to our future 'spiritual' life in the timeless eternity of Heaven, sheds a whole new light on the purpose of our earthly existence. In contrast to the materialistic atheist view that 'there is no ultimate purpose to our lives', we can view our time on Earth as a preparation for the rest of Eternity. It's while on Earth that we are meant to learn to love and to start to understand God's nature, purposes and goals.

Indeed, perhaps it helps explain why God isn't more 'obvious' to most of us; or, as we saw Bertrand Russell put it: "Not enough evidence, God, not enough evidence!" In the book "Partnering With God', I proposed that God has organised our life on Earth as a kind of 'problem-based learning' exercise—that:

> God hasn't given us all knowledge and understand-ing 'on a plate'…we have to search for God, follow-ing the clues and signposts that God provides. And, when we get a glimpse of God, we have to continue to reach out in order to find out more and to know God better. God has thus arranged things in this life so that it educates us and prepares us for life in God's eternal kingdom (where all will be known and understood). So, this life is a sort of 'training ground' in which being told too much too easily would be counter-productive for our education. We have to put in the effort—to face the challenges and solve the problems that bring us closer to God.[31]

You might counter all that's been discussed here by say-ing, "OK, accepting that God, the Afterlife and the human soul are 'real' based on reasonable evidence and testimony, is just an 'intellectual exercise'. It's a bit like accepting that Antarctica exists, although I've never been there myself. And this knowledge isn't going to have any effect on how I live my life!"

Well, yes, I can see the point of that argument. It's a bit like saying that a person can believe something intellectually without *feeling* its reality emotionally. This is, however, not at all uncommon and has, in fact, been the experience in the 'journey of faith' of some very prominent and influential Christians.

In Chapter 3, we mentioned the case of John Wesley, the eighteenth-century founder of the Methodist and Wesleyan Church Denominations. Even as an Anglican Preacher, Wesley felt that his faith was 'empty'—he didn't 'feel the reality' of God in his life. In fact, Wesley confessed to a friend that he was thinking of giving up preaching. In response his friend advised, "Preach faith till you have it. And then because you have faith, you will preach it!" Another way of putting this is, "Act as if you have faith, and it will be granted to you." And, as we saw in Chapter 3, this is exactly what happened to Wesley.

Another example is provided by the well-known writer and academic C.S. Lewis, who also became a prominent Christian apologist in the mid-twentieth century (we defined apologetics in Chapter 3). He's probably most famous for writing *The Lion, the Witch and the Wardrobe*, and the other books about Narnia. Lewis also wrote some widely read books on Christianity, including an autobiographical book entitled *Surprised by Joy*, in which he recounts his journey from atheism to Christianity. [32] However, this wasn't a straight forward journey! Lewis admitted to himself (and to God!) that he believed in God, one evening in 1929 in his room at Magdalene College, Oxford. However, this intellectual acceptance of the reality of God was transformed into a personal belief in Jesus Christ only two years later, following discussions with his friend J.R.R. Tolkien (who is well known for writing *The Hobbit* and *The Lord of the Rings*).

Although I certainly wouldn't presume to place myself in the same ballpark as Wesley or Lewis, I can say that my experience of the journey from intellectual belief to faith as a feeling of personal conviction has been similar.

You may feel that much of this book has been about death! But actually, I believe that it's all about life! It's about the meaning and purpose of our life here on Earth (that is, our physical, time-constrained life), how we can live it most fully—and how our Earthly life relates to, and continues into, our eternal spiritual life.

Let's end this chapter and Part 1 of this book with some words of another NDEr and what her NDE taught her about 'why we're here'. This is Mary Neal, an orthopaedic surgeon who underwent an NDE during a drowning accident while kayaking in Chile[33]. This is how Mary explained what she learned:

> *We need to be about God's business every moment of every day. …if you accept that there's life after death and … the rest of God's promises… it changes the way you see today…every moment matters, every choice, every decision…the reality is that we are here for a reason. We are here to learn and grow and change and help others do the same. …the only thing that truly matters is loving God and being a window through which God's light can shine through this world, and loving each other.[25]*

Mary Neal's words above reflect the central message of Christianity, starting with the words of Jesus himself 2000 years ago. If you'd like to explore this connection, then please turn the page and move on to Part 2 of this book.

Things To Think About
FOR REFLECTION AND DISCUSSION

---

1)   Do you agree with all (or any) of the six conclusions at the beginning of this Chapter?

2) Do you agree with the statement that 'the purpose of our life on Earth is to learn and to love'?

3) Why do you think that God isn't more 'obvious' to us?

4) Do you think that, in religious terms, there's a difference between 'intellectual belief' and 'personal faith'? Do you possess either (or both) of these?

5) What's your reaction to the concept that our physical life progresses into our spiritual life, with death being simply the demise of our physical body at the point of transition?

6) Do you wake up each morning thinking, 'I'm thankful for today—it really matters!'?

7) Do you know enough about any particular religion (e.g. Christianity) to see how the contents of Part 1 of this book relate to that religion's teachings?

8) Has reading Part 1 of this book, and reflecting on its contents, helped you think more about 'why you are here'?

Part 2

Introduction

A t the start of this book, I mentioned that I am a scientist and that I've spent my career undertaking research—generating and analysing experimental data in order to test hypotheses and understand more about the immune system. Perhaps it's partly for this reason that I'm particularly attracted to data that provides evidence that's consistent with there being a spiritual dimension to reality.

We've seen that Paradoxical Lucidity and OBEs provide evidence that is corroborated by independent observers. Although independent verification isn't possible for transcendent NDEs, we've seen that a strong argument can be made that these are real (rather than imagined) events.

I also mentioned that I'm a Christian, and that I find being both a scientist and a Christian to be entirely compatible.

Therefore, in Part 2 of this book, I aim to show the compatibility between the experiences of NDErs and the central message of Christianity—showing how many of the key features of NDEs are consistent with traditional Christian teachings of the past 2000 years.

This is not discounting compatibilities between NDEs and other religious traditions, but I don't have the background or knowledge to speak about these. As I proposed in Chapter 7, perhaps God's full and true nature is far beyond anything that can be fully comprehended by us mere mortals. Therefore, God meets us in ways that we can understand and cope with. This is related to the cultural and religious tradition in which we live. Thus, for me, the context in which I'm able to understand and interpret the religious significance of NDEs is Christianity.

The main textual source of information for Christians is the book known as the Bible—what you might call the core text of Christianity. In fact, the Bible is a compilation of at least sixty-six books written over a period of about 1,200 years by many different writers; and these books are not of just one type—there's history, prophesy, poetry, legal stuff, narrative, educational stories, parables, letters, revelations, and more!

The Bible is divided into two main parts. The first, larger part is known by Christians as The Old Testament. It was composed by Hebrew Jewish writers between about 1,200 and 165 years before the birth of Jesus and recounts the Hebrews' understanding of God and their relationship with Him, intertwined with the history of the Hebrew Nation.

The second part of the Bible is known as The New Testament and was written nearly 2,000 years ago by some of the earliest Christians in the 60 to 70 years following the earthly life of Jesus. This contains four accounts of the life and teachings of Jesus: these are known as the Gospels (which means "good news") and are named after the people who wrote them—Matthew, Mark, Luke and John. Luke also wrote the book that follows the Gospels, called The Acts of the Apostles, that describes the missionary work of some of the first teachers of the Christian faith (known as the Apostles). There are then numerous letters written by some of the Apostles to encourage the faith of their fellow Christians. Finally, there's a visionary book called The Book of Revelation.

You might ask, "If the experiences of NDErs are true insights into the reality of God and the Afterlife, why do NDEs seem to be modern events? Why haven't they been a feature of religious experiences for hundreds or thousands of years?"

Well, part of the answer is that NDEs are *not* just modern events, and that NDEs, or related transcendent religious experiences, *have* occurred in centuries past.

A possible example is provided by no less a person than Saint Paul, who was one of the greatest Apostles in the years following the earthly life of Jesus. Paul travelled widely around the Middle East and Southern Europe teaching about the 'Good News of Jesus Christ'. His missionary journeys are recounted in The Acts of the Apostle.

Paul also wrote many of the letters included in the New Testament: several of these were to Christian communities in cities that he had visited and in which he'd helped to convert people to Christianity. Paul's letters contain a mixture of teaching, guidance, encouragement and, sometimes, admonishment and warnings when he felt that some of these recently converted Christians were in danger of 'going astray'! Two of his letters were to the Christians in the Greek city of Corinth. In the second of these letters, Paul expresses concern that the Corinthian Christians are being subverted by the teachings of false apostles who were smooth talkers, and full of their own importance. So in response, and although reluctant to do so, Paul goes on to say:

> *You've forced me to talk this way, and I do it against my better judgment. But now that we're at it, I may as well bring up the matter of visions and revelations that God gave me. For instance, I know a man who, fourteen years ago, was seized by Christ and swept in ecstasy to the heights of heaven. I really don't know if this took place in the body or out of it; only God knows. I also know that this man was hijacked into paradise—again,*

whether in or out of the body, I don't know; God knows. There he heard the unspeakable spoken, but was forbidden to tell what he heard. This is the man I want to talk about. But about myself, I'm not saying another word apart from the humiliations.[34]

Although Paul chose to speak in the third person about being "swept in ecstasy to the heights of heaven" and "hijacked into Paradise," it seems probable that he was recounting his own experience, but not wishing to boast about it! What Paul describes bears many of the hallmarks of an NDE! We don't know for certain the circumstances of Paul's experience: he wrote his second letter to the Corinthians in about 56AD and says that the experience he describes occurred fourteen years earlier—so around 42AD. This might coincide with an incident described in The Acts of the Apostles that occurred in the town of Lystra when Paul was attacked and left for dead: "Then some Jews from Antioch and Iconium caught up with them and turned the fickle crowd against them. They beat Paul unconscious, dragged him outside the town and left him for dead. But as the disciples gathered around him, he came to and got up."[35]

If this was when Paul had his experience of being "swept in ecstasy to the heights of heaven," then it could, indeed, be classified as an NDE!

A second probable reason why NDEs seem to have become more common recently is related to scientific and medical advances in the past sixty years. For example, a significant proportion of NDEs occur in people who've had severe, life-threatening heart attacks. A few decades ago, this would cause the death of about half of these people. Today, however, over 90% of heart attack victims survive as a consequence of improvements in the treatment of heart attacks. Some of these people come close to death and may experience an NDE, whereas previously they were more likely to die and therefore not survive to recount an NDE.

In addition, and as mentioned in Chapter 5, systematic research into NDEs started only in the 1970s with a study by Raymond Moody.[8] This helped trigger further interest and scientific investigation of NDEs by an increasing number of clinicians and scientists. Thus, by 2020, thousands of NDEs had been reported and investigated, with the results of these studies published in many scientific journals and popular books.

So, what do NDEs of today share in common with the central message of the Bible and with the teachings of Jesus? Let's take a look…

Chapter 10

Light

"There's light at the end of the tunnel." That's a well-known phrase often used to mean that, after a period of difficulty, anxiety or other type of stress in a person's life, they can finally see that things are getting better.

An appreciation of light seems to be intrinsic to our nature. And this is not just in relation to the physical effects of light, but also its association with positive emotions—feelings of hope, joy, contentment, optimism and so on.

For many people (including me) who live a long way from the Equator, one of the key things we appreciate about Summer are the length of the days, with the sun rising early in the morning and setting late in the evening. Indeed, for those who live far enough North or South, the sun never sets around the time of the Summer Solstice (i.e. the longest day).

Conversely, the downside of living where the mid-summer days are very long is that the mid-winter days are very short—there are more hours of dark than of light!

This yearly cycle of light and dark has been an important feature of religious festivals around the world for thousands of years. For example, on the flat, open landscape of Salisbury Plain in Southern England stands the impressive Neolithic Monument known as Stonehenge. Built around 4,500 years ago from massive stones, some weighing 20-35 tonnes, it's an incredible feat of Stone Age engineering. What's more, the whole structure was precisely aligned so that, on the day of the Summer Solstice, the Sun would rise above a particular stone called the Heel Stone. And, probably more importantly to those who built Stonehenge, 180 degrees in the opposite direction to the Heel Stone, on the day of the Winter Solstice (the shortest day), the evening Sun would sink between the two largest and heaviest stones, and set over the central Altar Stone. After this, the days started to get longer again and the position of the setting Sun would change, indicating that Spring was on the way. Marking the times of greatest light and least light, as well as the associated change of the seasons, probably had enormous spiritual, as well as practical, significance for these primeval farmers.

The Hindu festival of Diwali, which takes place in late October-November, is known as the 'Festival of Lights'. Diwali represents the "spiritual victory of light over darkness, good over evil, and knowledge over ignorance".

The Romans celebrated Sol Invictus (the "unconquered sun") on 25th December (around the time of the Winter Solstice)—it's thought that this may be why early Christians chose this date to celebrate the birth of Jesus Christ—that is, Christmas.

This appreciation of light throughout the history of humanity, and our instinctive understanding of its deep-rooted significance, is emphasised still further by the experiences of the NDErs discussed in Part 1.

In Chapter 6, we considered how Bill Herlund, in common with many other NDErs, literally saw 'light at the end of the tunnel' that he passed through as his soul travelled from Earth to a Heavenly Dimension. As he approached the light, Bill realised that it emanated from a 'Light Being' who also radiated love and peace.[14] This is reminiscent of Samaa's description of her encounter with Jesus during her NDE that was precipitated by the blast of a terrorist's bomb in the church where she was worshipping (Chapter 7). She said that Jesus' face "was brighter than the sun" and that "He radiated an amazing love that contained deep acceptance."[24]

In a very similar way, Dean Braxton encountered Jesus during an NDE and described him thus: "Jesus is pure light! His brightness was before me, around me, part of me and within me. He is brighter than the noonday sun, but we can still look at Him in Heaven."[36]

The nature of the light that illuminates Heaven itself is also particularly striking to many NDErs, and features prominently in their accounts. Brad Barrows (Chapter 6) was blind from birth and so had never 'seen' light until freed from his sightless body during an NDE. Having passed through a tunnel, he reported finding himself "in an immense field illuminated by a tremendous, all-encompassing light."[18]

Similarly, Dale Black, an airline pilot who underwent an NDE when a small plane in which he was a passenger crashed, recalled the light he experienced as he approached what he described as a Heavenly City:

> The entire city was bathed in light, an opaque whiteness in which the light was intense but diffused. In that dazzling light every colour imaginable seemed to exist.... The colours seemed to be alive, dancing in the air... Oddly, [the light] didn't make me squint to look at it... The light was palpable. It had substance to it, weight and thickness, like nothing I had ever seen before or since.... Somehow, I knew that light and life and love were connected and interrelated.[37]

Since prehistoric times, humans have associated light with goodness, love and well-being, and have associated darkness with evil, hate and destruction. This is reflected in the religious festivals across many cultures (some of which were mentioned above) that celebrate the triumph of light over darkness.

This is again reflected in NDE accounts where, as highlighted above, those who undergo positive, heavenly NDEs frequently are awestruck by the amazing light to which they are exposed. By contrast, as exemplified by the account of Ian McCormack's NDE in Chapter 7, darkness can be a key feature of negative, hellish NDEs. Furthermore, those rescued from such experiences, as in Ian's case, are again often struck by their transition from a place of darkness to a place of pure light. As Ian said: "a brilliant light shone upon me and literally drew me out of the darkness. A voice spoke to me from the centre of the light": 'Ian, you must see in a new light.'"[28]

The importance of light in the positive experiences of NDErs is reflected in the symbolic role of light throughout the history of Judaism and Christianity, and as recorded in the Bible.

The first book of the Bible is called Genesis, which means 'origins', and it begins with a poetic description of the Creation. This is how it starts: *"In the beginning when God created the heavens and the earth, the earth was a formless void and darkness covered the face of the deep, while a wind from God swept over the face of the waters. Then God said, "Let there be light"; and there was light. And God saw that the light was good."*[38] So, according to this ancient biblical narrative of Creation, light was the first thing that God made! Of course, most scientists these days agree that the universe started with the 'Big Bang' about 13.8 billion years ago, and that the Earth started to form just 4.5 billion years ago. However, it's likely that a massive explosion of light accompanied the Big Bang!

In the Old Testament, the Book of Psalms is a collection of Jewish hymns, written over many centuries. Some of these refer to 'light' and contrast it with 'darkness'. For example, Psalm 18 contains the line, *"O Lord, you give me light; you dispel my darkness."*[39] And in Psalm 27: *"The Lord is my light and my salvation."*[40]

The Old Testament also contains numerous Books of the Prophets. In the Jewish tradition, the prophets were people called by God to proclaim God's message to the Jews. Sometimes the message was one of hope and God's faithfulness but, at other times, the message contained warnings because of the way that people had wandered away from God. The book of the prophet Isaiah contains the following message of hope: *"The people who walked in darkness have seen a great light. They lived in a land of shadows, but now light is shining on them."*[41] Indeed, Matthew repeats this message in his New Testament Gospel as a prophesy referring to the coming of Jesus[42]. John's Gospel also attributes the following words to Jesus: "...*Jesus spoke to them, saying, 'I am the light of the world. Whoever follows me will never walk in darkness but will have the light of life.'*"[43]

Christians regard Jesus as 'God in human form'—hence giving Jesus the title 'Christ', which means 'the Chosen One'. Another way of looking at this is to say, "If you want to know what God is like, then look at what Jesus was like—what he said and did." This relationship between God and Jesus is actually apparent in the context of Light that we're considering here. We saw above that, with regard to his NDE, Dean Braxton said, "Jesus is pure light!"[36] Two thousand years ago in his first Letter, John described God in exactly the same way:

> *This, in essence, is the message we heard from Christ and are passing on to you: God is light, pure light; there's not a trace of darkness in him. If we claim that we experience a shared life with him and continue to stumble around in the dark, we're obviously lying... we're not living what we claim. But if we walk in the light, God himself being the light, we also experience a shared life with one another...*[44]

An important event during Jesus' ministry, that's recorded in three of the four Gospels, is what's known as the

'Transfiguration'. This is how it's described in Matthew's Gospel:

> *Jesus took with him Peter and the brothers James and John and led them up a high mountain where they were alone. As they looked on, a change came over Jesus: his face was shining like the sun, and his clothes were dazzling white. Then the three disciples saw Moses and Elijah talking with Jesus.*[45]

Moses was a leader of the Hebrews who led them out of slavery in Egypt about 1300 years before the time of Jesus; Elijah was an important Jewish prophet about 900 years before Jesus. However, what's remarkable about this event as recounted by the disciples who accompanied Jesus up that mountain, is not only the meeting with Moses and Elijah, but that Jesus himself was changed (i.e. transfigured), so that *"his face was shining like the sun, and his clothes were dazzling white."*[45] This is exactly how NDErs describe Jesus in their encounters with him, as we've seen above in the accounts of Samaa Habib and Dean Braxton.

We saw in Chapter 7 that, for many NDErs, their transcendent experience leads to a change in their spiritual values and an enhanced sense of mission or purpose in their lives. This includes a desire to share their new-found knowledge of

God with others. This sense of mission is again reflected in the Bible. For example, in his first Letter, the Apostle Peter gave this message to the Christians to whom he was writing: *"But you are the chosen race, the King's priests, the holy nation, God's own people, chosen to proclaim the wonderful acts of God, who called you out of darkness into his own marvellous light."*[46]

Indeed, Jesus told his followers that they, themselves, should act as 'lights to the world' in providing an example of how God wants us to live: *"You are like light for the whole world. A city built on a hill cannot be hid. No one lights a lamp and puts it under a bowl; instead it is put on the lampstand, where it gives light for everyone in the house. In the same way your light must shine before people, so that they will see the good things you do and praise your Father in heaven."*[47]

Many NDErs would agree with this light-based analogy as a statement of their purpose.

Things To Think About
FOR REFLECTION AND DISCUSSION

---

1) What feelings and emotions do you associate with light?

2) What do you like, and dislike, about mid-Summer and mid-Winter?

3) How do you feel when you see a beautiful sunrise or sunset? Are your feelings different in these two cases?
4) Do you think the religious associations of light are real, or just symbolic?
5) Why do we associate light with goodness and darkness with evil?

Chapter 11

Love

In July 1967, when I was twelve years old, there was the first ever global television broadcast, which was called 'Our World'. The programme was watched by over 400 million people in 25 countries. What I still remember about that programme, all these years later, is the British contribution. This was the Beatles giving the first public performance of their song, written by John Lennon, 'All You Need is Love'. You can still watch that original recording on the World Wide Web which, of course, didn't exist in 1967! [48]

But what does 'love' really mean? It forms the central theme of countless novels, poems, plays, films, songs, paintings…and has done so ever since humans found ways of expressing their emotions artistically. In many instances, of course, these are expressions of what we might call romantic love or, indeed, sexual love.

But we all know that this is just one form of love—the love that a person has for a 'life partner' is much more than just their sexual relationship; and this is different again from the forms of love we feel for our parents, siblings, children, friends. Furthermore, what do we mean when we say we love our work, or we love a particular painting or song, or we love being by the sea or watching the sun set?

Going further, how can we be sure that God loves us?

There's a children's hymn that I recall singing in Sunday School that begins "Jesus loves me, this I know, for the Bible tells me so…" That, indeed, is key for many Christians: over and over again the Bible speaks of God's love for each and every one of us. We'll come back to that further on in this chapter.

Another key factor for many Christians is that they 'feel' God's love for them. We touched on this in Chapter 3, and acknowledged that for those who have no sense of God's presence, let alone God's love, it's hard for them to understand this.

So, perhaps it might help to look again at what NDErs have to say about their experience of God's love.

What we find is that many NDErs report that they were overwhelmed not only by God's (or Jesus') radiant light (discussed in the previous chapter), but also by God (or Jesus) radiating love for them.

For example, Bill Herlund (Chapter 6) reported that the 'Light Being' he encountered after being hit by the explosive blast from a burning aircraft, "radiated unconditional love and peace."[14]

The blind NDEr, Brad Barrows (Chapter 6), said that the man he encountered (and could see!) "emanated an overwhelming love."[18]

Samaa Habib (Chapter 7), caught in the blast of a terrorist's bomb, reported that when she met Jesus, he "radiated an amazing love that contained deep acceptance."[24]

Rajiv Parti (Chapter 7) said that, as he was enveloped by the brightness of the Being of Light, "…pure love…pervaded everything, as if my five earthly senses were soaked in omniscient, all-powerful love."[13]

Even Ian McCormack (Chapter 7), lethally stung by box jellyfish, and who knew that he'd rejected God during his life, was rescued by God from utter darkness and, to his amazement, he said, "a wave of pure unconditional love flowed over me…Instead of judgement I was being washed in pure love."[28]

These are just a handful from hundreds, if not thousands, of examples in which NDErs have witnessed to God's love for them, and which they experienced to its full extent when stood before God. Furthermore, each one not only refers to God's love, but describes this love as "unconditional," "overwhelming," "amazing," "pure"... and so on. In other words, it's a love far greater and deeper than anything they've previously experienced or can fully comprehend or explain.

In chapter 7, I mentioned Howard Storm who, like Ian McCormack, underwent a distressing NDE that was transformed into one of joy when he appealed to Jesus for help. This is how Howard described the love of Jesus that he felt as Jesus carried him out of the place of despair: "I experienced love in such intensity that nothing I had ever known before was comparable. His love was greater than all human love put together. His love totally enveloped me...He was more loving than one can begin to imagine or describe. Jesus did indeed love me."[29]

These first-hand descriptions of God's love by modern-day NDErs reflect how the writers of scripture described God's love thousands of years ago.

For example, in his first letter, the apostle John wrote, *"And so we know and rely on the love God has for us.* **God is love.** *Whoever lives in love lives in God, and God in them."*[49] Thus, John indicates that love is so intrinsic to God's nature that John simply says *"God is love."*[49] We saw, in Chapter 9, that this understanding of God's love was echoed by the NDEr Crystal McVea when she tried to find the right words to describe her encounter with God: "He is a loving God. I realized I didn't just love God. I realized He IS love."[30]

This is also expressed by Rajiv Parti who reported that one of the angels he encountered described the love associated with the Being of Light thus: "…this pure love is the base reality, the underlying fabric, of everything in the universe. It is the source of all creation, the creative force of the universe."[13]

You may have heard God described as being 'omnipotent'. This means 'all-powerful'—in Latin, *omni* means 'all' and *potens* means 'powerful'. However, the theologian Thomas Jay Oord has proposed that a better word to describe God's essential nature is 'amipotence.'[50] The prefix 'ami' is derived from the Latin word for love—*amor*. Thus, amipotence describes God as supremely possessing and expressing His power as love. This certainly aligns with God's nature as portrayed in the Bible. It also resonates with the experience of God reported by NDErs.

The Bible not only speaks of the power of God's love, but also of its constancy. In other words, God's love is unwavering and forever. This is particularly found in references to God's love in the Old Testament. For example, the Book of Deuteronomy says: *"Remember that the Lord your God is the only God and that he is faithful. He will keep his covenant and show his constant love to a thousand generations of those who love him and obey his commands."*[51] Of course, this isn't suggesting that God will stop loving after a thousand generations! It's just a poetic way of saying that God's love will go on and on.

Similarly, in the Psalms we find the following verses: *"Your constant love is better than life itself, and so I will praise You,"*[52] and *"But You, O LORD, are a merciful and loving God, always patient, always kind and faithful."*[53]

And the following translation of a verse from the Book of the prophet Jeremiah really brings the point home: "God told them, 'I've never [stopped] loving you and never will. Expect love, love and more love!'"[54]

Although not everyone gets to experience God's love during this life as powerfully as described in the NDE accounts above, Christians believe that the best example we have of God's love is provided in the life of Jesus. Indeed, in his Gospel, the apostle John says in one of the best known of verses from the Bible: *"For God loved the world so much that he gave his only Son, so that everyone who believes in him may not die but have eternal life"*[55]. And Jesus himself said: *"My commandment is this: love one another, just as I love you."*[56]

But what can we expect of God's love for us, apart from it being the strongest and most constant love possible? In what ways does God love us?

In his first letter to the Corinthians, the apostle Paul describes the nature of love thus: *"Love is patient and kind;*

love does not envy or boast; it is not arrogant or rude. It does not insist on its own way; it is not irritable or resentful; it does not rejoice at wrongdoing, but rejoices with the truth. Love bears all things, believes all things, hopes all things, endures all things. Love never ends."[57]

In his book *Pluriform Love*, Thomas Jay Oord points out that the New Testament was originally written in Greek, and that three different Greek words are used, all of which are translated in English as 'love'.[58] These three Greek words are *agape, eros* and *philia*. Oord helpfully explains that *agape* can be thought of as 'in spite of love'—for example, loving someone who's not easy to love. *Eros* is 'because of love'—such as loving someone who also gives love. *Philia* is 'alongside of love'—for example, supporting someone in a loving way. The main point is that God loves all of us, all of the time, in all of these ways, and more!

The unquenchable and all-pervading nature of God's love is beautifully summed up by the Apostle Paul in his letter to Christians in Rome when he said: *"...I am convinced that neither death, nor life, nor angels, nor rulers, nor things present, nor things to come, nor powers, nor height, nor depth, nor anything else in all creation, will be able to separate us from the love of God in Christ Jesus our Lord."*[59]

So, in this Chapter we've considered God's love for us. But what about our love for God and for each other? Indeed, in another verse in his first letter, John again says that 'God is love', but puts it like this: *"Whoever does not love does not know God, because God is love."*[60]

We'll return to think more about how *we* should love in Chapter 13.

However, in the next Chapter, we'll consider one of the most important and amazing consequences of God's love for us—and that's God's forgiveness.

Things To Think About
FOR REFLECTION AND DISCUSSION

---

1) Who and what do you love the most?
2) Can you think of times when you have given or received agape ('in spite of' love), eros ('because of' love), philia ('alongside of' love)?
3) If God's primary concern was to exercise control rather than to express love, what difference would this make to the world and to our lives?
4) Have you ever directly experienced God's love? If so, how do you know, and how does it feel?
5) Why do you think some people regard love as a weakness rather than as a strength?

Chapter 12

Forgiveness

Even if they know nothing else about the life of Jesus, the one thing that most people are likely to know is how Jesus died—that he was crucified.

Crucifixion was used by the Romans as a particularly slow, painful and humiliating form of execution. It thus made the process of dying as unpleasant as possible for the victim. It also served as a warning to any who witnessed this gruesome process who might themselves be tempted to perpetrate a crime similar to that of which the person being crucified was accused.

In Jesus' case, however, he hadn't committed any crime. Indeed, quite the opposite! He'd spent his life and ministry showing and teaching love, doing good, healing the sick and befriending the outcasts of society. However, this had brought him into conflict with the Jewish religious leaders. They saw Jesus as a threat to their authority and were aware that he criticised and undermined their values and self-importance.

It was thus these leaders of Jesus' own community who wanted him killed—not the Roman rulers. Indeed, Pontius Pilate, the Roman Governor of Palestine, recognised that Jesus was innocent of any crime. Pilate wanted to release Jesus, but some of the Jewish population had been whipped up into such a state of hatred against Jesus by their leaders that Pilate decided to let them have their way. Thus, Pilate allowed Jesus to be crucified simply to appease the mob and avoid a riot.

So how did Jesus react? Was he frightened, furious, protesting his innocence, pleading for mercy and that his life should be spared? No—none of these reactions. But, as he was raised aloft on the cross to which he'd been nailed, Jesus said: *"Forgive them, Father! They don't know what they are doing."*[61]

There are numerous theories about the true significance of Jesus' crucifixion. Christians believe that Jesus deliberately sacrificed his life for humankind. He knew full well that the Jewish religious leaders wanted him killed, and he did not try to avoid his execution. Indeed, he seemed to be fully aware that this would be the outcome of his final trip to Jerusalem. Furthermore, Jesus indicated that his sacrificial death was essential to the purpose of his ministry—his final words at the moment of his death on the cross were: *"It is finished."*[62]

Within 40 hours of his death, Christians believe that Jesus was alive again. This, of course, seems impossible and unbelievable to many. However, some NDE accounts actually cast doubt on such doubts!

For example, Mary Neal, who was mentioned at the end of Chapter 9, underwent her NDE when completely submerged underwater in her kayak for 14 minutes before her body broke free and came to the surface of the river. This is far longer than a normal person should be able to survive without oxygen, and yet Mary made a full recovery.[33]

Indeed, we are told in the Gospels that, on two occasions, Jesus brought a dead person back to life. One was the daughter of a man called Jairus,[63] and the other was a friend of Jesus' called Lazarus.[64] These are just two examples of the many miracles performed by Jesus that are recounted in the Gospels. Miracles can be defined as good events that appear to defy the laws of nature, as we understand them. According to this definition, it seems reasonable to define the recovery of Mary Neal (and some other NDErs) as miraculous![33]

But let's return to thinking about Jesus' death on the cross and his words *"Forgive them, Father! They don't know what they are doing."*[61]

What could be worse than killing God's own Son? Well, probably nothing. And yet, even this could be forgiven by God. In other words, there are no bad things (commonly called 'sins') we can do that God can't—or won't—forgive. Thus, God's love and forgiveness overcomes all our wrong-doing (i.e. 'sinfulness'). Christians believe that this is demonstrated supremely by Jesus' submission to crucifixion and his subsequent resurrection.

This is how the apostle Paul put it in his letter to the Christians in the city of Colossae: "*When you were stuck in your old sin-dead life, you were incapable of responding to God. God brought you alive—right along with Christ! Think of it! All sins forgiven, the slate wiped clean, that old arrest warrant cancelled and nailed to Christ's cross.*"[65]

As described in previous chapters, the accounts of NDErs reflect this experience of God's limitless capacity for forgiveness.

We've seen that many NDErs undergo a 'life review' that concentrates on the way that they've treated others during their life—both good and bad. Bill Herlund (chapter 6), for example, described how his encounter with a 'Light Being' included a life review and that "*I was not proud of some of my dealings with other people, but the light was quick to forgive all of my errors.*"[14]

Similarly, Rene Hope Turner (chapter 8) recounted that during a review of her 'life's less complimentary moments,'

"I relived those moments and felt not only what I had done but also the hurt I had caused…When I became burdened with guilt I was directed to other events which gave joy to others…I received great Love."[27]

When Crystal McVea felt that she'd let God down during her time on Earth (chapter 9), she discovered that *"…God wouldn't allow me to feel bad about it. There is no feeling bad in heaven…He is a loving God."*[30]

Rajiv Parti (Chapter 7) said that, when his Life Review had ended, *"I felt small and full of shame…But rather than receiving something bad, I felt a deep sense of love coming from the Being of Light…"*[13]

Ian McCormack (chapter 7), who'd deliberately turned his back on God during his life, but appealed to God for forgiveness when he was stung to death by box jellyfish, recounted that, *"To my amazement a wave of pure unconditional love flowed over me…Instead of judgement I was being washed with pure love. Pure, unadulterated, clean, uninhibited, undeserved, love."*[28]

Similarly, Howard Storm (chapter 7), who also rejected God prior to his NDE in which Jesus rescued him from a distressing situation, explained what he was told about God's forgiveness thus:

It is very important that you understand God's forgiveness. When you ask God to forgive and you

mean it from the heart, you are forgiven…God
wants you to be full of joy, and grow into a wonderful child of God. God doesn't want us to carry guilt.
God wants us to develop to our full potential as
creative, joyful, participants in the creation. When
we ask God's forgiveness it is given.[29]

An important point that Howard Storm makes here,
and is also made in many verses from the Bible, is that God
won't force his forgiveness on us! We have to want it and
accept it—we have to say sorry and show repentance (i.e.
change our ways). We'll return to this point in Chapter 14.

There are many verses in the Bible that speak of God's
limitless capacity for forgiveness. For example, an Old
Testament Psalm says: *"You, Lord, are forgiving and good,
abounding in love to all who call to you."*[66]

We saw earlier in this chapter some verses from the
apostle Paul's letter to the Colossians. At another point in
the same letter, Paul states: *"He rescued us from the power of
darkness and brought us safe into the kingdom of his dear Son,
by whom we are set free, that is, our sins are forgiven."*[67]

And in his first letter in the New Testament, the apostle
John wrote: *"…if we confess our sins to God, he will keep his
promise and do what is right: he will forgive us our sins and
purify us from all our wrongdoing."*[68]

However, one of the best known passages in the Bible about forgiveness is not a statement, such as those above from the letters of Paul and John—it's known as the Parable of the Prodigal (or Lost) Son.

Parables are short stories that Jesus told in order to illustrate what God is like and what God wants us to do. The word 'prodigal' is not often heard these days, but what it means is 'to use money or resources recklessly and wastefully.' You'll see why the son in this parable that Jesus told is called 'prodigal' or 'lost!'

> "There was once a man who had two sons. The younger one said to him, 'Father, give me my share of the property now.' So the man divided his property between his two sons. After a few days the younger son sold his part of the property and left home with the money. He went to a country far away, where he wasted his money in reckless living. He spent everything he had. Then a severe famine spread over that country, and he was left without a thing. So he went to work for one of the citizens of that country, who sent him out to his farm to take care of the pigs. He wished he could fill himself with the bean pods the pigs ate, but no one gave him anything to eat. At last he came to his senses and said, 'All my father's hired workers have more than

they can eat, and here I am about to starve! I will get up and go to my father and say, 'Father, I have sinned against God and against you. I am no longer fit to be called your son; treat me as one of your hired workers.' So he got up and started back to his father. He was still a long way from home when his father saw him; his heart was filled with pity, and he ran, threw his arms around his son, and kissed him. 'Father,' the son said, 'I have sinned against God and against you. I am no longer fit to be called your son.' But the father called to his servants. 'Hurry!' he said. 'Bring the best robe and put it on him. Put a ring on his finger and shoes on his feet. Then go and get the prize calf and kill it, and let us celebrate with a feast! For this son of mine was dead, but now he is alive; he was lost, but now he has been found.' And so the feasting began.[69]

In this parable we can consider that the 'father' represents God, and the 'son' represents any of us. The father didn't reject his son or even scold him. Instead, the father was so overjoyed at his son's return and repentance that he immediately welcomed his son fully back into his family. The parable thus gives us a clear and memorable message about God's infinite capacity for love and forgiveness.

Things To Think About

FOR REFLECTION AND DISCUSSION

1) Are there times when you feel the need for forgiveness?

2) Are there times when you find it hard to forgive others?

3) How easy is it to believe that God will always forgive us if we're sorry and repent for our wrong-doing?

4) Do you think that God ever gets frustrated with our failings?

5) Why do you think that the Cross is the pre-eminent Christian symbol?

Chapter 13

Purpose

We've spoken in previous chapters about the journeys of the apostle Paul around Eastern Europe and the Middle East in order to tell people about Jesus' Gospel message. On one occasion, Paul visited Athens—the most academic and intellectually active city of his day. While there, Paul got into a debate with some Greek philosophers during which he argued as follows: "... *[God] created all races of people and made them live throughout the whole earth. He himself fixed beforehand the exact times and the limits of the places where they would live. He did this so that they would look for him, and perhaps find him as they felt around for him. Yet God is actually not far from any one of us...*"[70]

Thus, Paul is saying that the purpose of our time here on planet Earth is to "seek and find God!" And when we find God, we can begin to understand, and to implement, his purposes for us.

So what is it that God wants us to do? What *is* our purpose?

Well, of course, we've already looked at this in chapter 9 at the end of Part 1 of this book. But let's consider it a little further here—after all, what could be more important?!

You may well have seen the classic Disney film of *The Jungle Book*, which includes the well-known song 'I wanna be like you'. In the film, this is sung by an orangutan who wants to be like a human. But the statement 'I wanna be like you' is also pertinent to our purpose in life!

What I mean by this is that those who 'find God', as described above by Paul, then want to be more like God, which means living a life more like that of Jesus.

Paul makes this clear in his letter to the Ephesians, in which he says: *"Since you are God's dear children, you must try to be like Him."*[71]

So what does it mean to 'be like God'? Well, we've seen in Chapters 11 and 12 that the two aspects of God's nature that are most striking to NDErs when they meet God (or Jesus), are His love and forgiveness. And this is often then reflected in how NDErs live the rest of their Earthly lives: they are more loving and forgiving to others—they are 'more like God'.

This is exactly what Paul goes on to say in the next sentence of his letter to the Ephesians: *"Your life must be controlled by love, just as Christ loved us…"*[72]

Indeed, Jesus himself said the very same to his disciples: *"And now I give you a new commandment: love one another. As I have loved you, so you must love one another. If you have love for one another, then everyone will know that you are my disciples."*[73]

You may recall from Chapter 9 that this is the central message that Mary Neal brought back following her NDE when she drowned during a kayaking accident. What Mary learned is that "We are here to learn and grow and change and help others do the same. …the only thing that truly matters is loving God and being a window through which God's light can shine through this world, and loving each other."[25]

We also saw in Chapter 8 that Howard Storm received this same message during his NDE. Howard recounted, "[Jesus] said, '…Your purpose is to love the person that you're with.'…If you love the person that you're with, they'll love the person that they're with and they'll love the person that they're with. And that will multiply… it's God's plan. It will work. Just love the person that you're with."[25]

This message is also stated simply, but beautifully, in the words of the well-known children's song "Magic Penny":

"Love is something if you give it away… You end up having more."[74]

Obviously, we all have many aspects to our lives: we have to make a living, provide for our families, fulfil obligations, pursue our interests. But God hasn't given us life just for it to be a matter of survival or 'making do'. Indeed, the purpose of our lives isn't even just trying to be happy—particularly if we fall into the trap of thinking that happiness is to be found through possessions, prestige, power or fame—those things don't bring lasting happiness.

Jesus put our purpose very simply, in a single sentence, when he said: *"Do for others what you want them to do for you: this is the meaning of the Law of Moses and of the teachings of the prophets."*[75] Thus, Jesus is saying that all the Jewish teachings written in the Old Testament of the Bible can be summed up in the single sentence, *"Do for others what you want them to do for you."*

Jesus' brother, James, refers to this in his letter that's included in the New Testament of the Bible: *"You do well when you complete the Royal Rule of the Scriptures: 'Love others as you love yourself.'"*[76]

This "Royal Rule", as James calls it, is often also known as The Golden Rule. I referred to it briefly in Chapter 8. It is central not only to Christianity and Judaism, but also to all the major religions of the world. For example:

In Islam: *"Not one of you truly believes until you wish for others what you wish for yourself"*[77]

In Hinduism: *"This is the sum of duty: do not do to others what would cause pain if done to you."*[78]

In Buddhism: *"Treat not others in ways that you yourself would find hurtful."*[79]

In Taoism: *"Regard your neighbour's gain as your own gain, and your neighbour's loss as your own loss."*[80]

Jesus, however, went further in explaining what the full implementation of the Golden Rule really means. This is recounted in Matthew's Gospel where Jesus says:

You have heard that it was said, 'Love your friends, hate your enemies.' But now I tell you: love your enemies and pray for those who persecute you, so that you may become the children of your Father in heaven. For he makes his sun to shine on bad and good people alike, and gives rain to those who do good and to those who do evil. Why should God reward you if you love only the people who love you?... And if you speak only to your friends, have you done anything out of the ordinary?...

*You must be perfect—just as your Father in heaven is
perfect.*[81]

Jesus also applied the same reasoning to forgiveness.
This is an exchange that took place between Jesus and Peter,
one of his disciples: *"Peter came to Jesus and asked, 'Lord, if my
brother keeps on sinning against me, how many times do I have
to forgive him? Seven times?' 'No, not seven times,' answered
Jesus, 'but seventy times seven.'"*[82] Seventy times seven is, of
course, 490. However, Jesus clearly wasn't saying that on
the 491st occasion, Peter shouldn't forgive! What he meant
was that we should always forgive wrongs done to us, just
(as we saw in Chapter 12) God's capacity for forgiveness is
limitless.

Jesus memorably illustrated the full meaning of the
Golden Rule in what is probably his best-known parable—
the Parable of the Good Samaritan. This is how it's recounted in Luke's Gospel:

*A teacher of the Law came up and tried to trap Jesus.
'Teacher,' he asked, 'what must I do to receive eternal
life?' Jesus answered him, 'What do the Scriptures say?
How do you interpret them?' The man answered, 'Love
the Lord your God with all your heart, with all your
soul, with all your strength, and with all your mind';*

and 'Love your neighbour as you love yourself.' 'You are right,' Jesus replied; 'do this and you will live.' But the teacher of the Law wanted to justify himself, so he asked Jesus, 'Who is my neighbour?' Jesus answered, 'There was once a man who was going down from Jerusalem to Jericho when robbers attacked him, stripped him, and beat him up, leaving him half dead. It so happened that a priest was going down that road; but when he saw the man, he walked on by on the other side. In the same way a Levite also came there, went over and looked at the man, and then walked on by on the other side. But a Samaritan who was traveling that way came upon the man, and when he saw him, his heart was filled with pity. He went over to him, poured oil and wine on his wounds and bandaged them; then he put the man on his own animal and took him to an inn, where he took care of him. The next day he took out two silver coins and gave them to the innkeeper. 'Take care of him,' he told the innkeeper, 'and when I come back this way, I will pay you whatever else you spend on him.' And Jesus concluded, 'In your opinion, which one of these three acted like a neighbour toward the man attacked by the robbers?' The teacher of the Law answered, 'The one who was kind to him.' Jesus replied, 'You go, then, and do the same.'[83]

An important aspect of this parable is that the two holy men—the Priest and the Levite—did not show kindness to the injured victim. By contrast, the one who did show kindness and, indeed, love, was a Samaritan, i.e. from the land of Samaria. The Jews who lived in the Kingdom of Judea looked down on the Samaritans, who they considered to be a 'fallen race' who had abandoned the true Jewish Faith. And yet it was the Samaritan, while knowing that he was despised, even hated, by many Jews, who showed love for the injured Jew. He didn't see an enemy lying by the roadside whose misfortune he could celebrate; he saw a fellow human being in distress, who needed his love and compassion. That's the Golden Rule in action.

Things To Think About

FOR REFLECTION AND DISCUSSION

1) During an average day, how often do you think of the people that you meet as your 'neighbour' to whom you should show kindness and love?

2) Which people do you find most difficult to think of as your neighbour?

3) Is love the most powerful force in the world? If so, why? If not, what is?

4) What prevents people from living their lives according to the 'Golden Rule'?

5) Christians have been persecuted for their faith throughout history. How may the teachings of Jesus help them to cope with this?

6) If love is not your purpose in life, what is?

Chapter 14

Choice

If you like statistical trivia, you'll be interested in this: there are three people whose names appear in the Bible far more than any others.[84] You probably won't be surprised to learn that the first of these is Jesus, whose name is mentioned 1,281 times. The second is David, with 971 mentions. King David is the most famous monarch of the Israelites, who lived about 1,000 years before Jesus. If you know nothing else about David, you probably know that, as a boy, he killed the Philistine giant Goliath with a sling-shot.

However, it's the third person on this list that I want to talk about here (with 803 mentions in the Bible), and that's Moses. He lived about 300 years before King David and is famous for being the leader and prophet who led the Israelites out of slavery in Egypt. The Israelites then lived as nomads in the wilderness of Sinai for 40 years, with Moses as their leader, until they felt ready to occupy the land of Canaan (that became Israel) where their ancestors Abraham, Isaac and Jacob had lived about 300-400 years earlier.

Moses didn't live to see the Israelites enter the land of Canaan. But shortly before he died, he offered the Israelites the following choice: *"I am now giving you the choice between life and death, between God's blessing and God's curse, and I call heaven and earth to witness the choice you make. Choose life. Love the Lord your God, obey him and be faithful to him, and then you and your descendants will live long in the land that he promised to give your ancestors, Abraham, Isaac, and Jacob."*[85]

Following the death of Moses, it was Joshua who led the Israelites across the River Jordan into the land of Canaan, which they conquered and in which they settled. Joshua (whose name appears 219 time in the Bible), then again offered the Israelites this choice: *"...honour the Lord and serve him sincerely and faithfully... If you are not willing to serve him, decide today whom you will serve, the gods your ancestors worshipped in Mesopotamia or the gods of the Amorites, in whose land you are now living. As for my family and me, we will serve the Lord."*[86]

What's striking about both of these proposals from Moses and Joshua is that they are not delivered as commands. They did not say to the Israelites, "You must worship God—you have no other option". Rather, they say, "You must choose whether you will worship God, or not—the choice is yours."

This tells us something very important about God's relationship with Creation in general, and with humans in particular: we have freedom to choose.

This freedom of choice is also illustrated in some NDE accounts when it comes to the choice for the NDEr whether or not to return to their earthly body.

Here's how Samaa Habib described how she made this choice:

'Do you want to go back or stay here in heaven?' Jesus asked… Then He showed me another scene—my whole family, some of whom weren't saved yet. Finally I saw myself, dead from the bomb blast, and then glimpsed my parents', siblings' and other relatives' reactions. It broke my heart to see their pain… Everything in me wanted to stay forever… But He is…a Gentleman. He never forced me but gave me the freedom to choose. As I told Him my choice—that I wanted to go back to earth and be a witness for Him—I was motivated by love, not a sense of duty… 'All right, see you soon,' He said.[24]

Crystal McVea also wanted to stay with God during her NDE, but then she heard her mother's voice, calling her name:

> 'I need to tell my mother I'm okay,' I said. And God responded. 'The choice is up to you.' I didn't want to leave God. I didn't want to go anywhere. I just wanted to let my mother know I was okay… As I turned away from the entrance to heaven, there was another communication from God—the last and most powerful thing He said to me. 'Tell them what you can remember.'[30]

It was being reminded of his mother that also persuaded Ian McCormack to return from his NDE[28]. Having been rescued from the "pit of darkness" and finding himself on the edge of paradise, Ian was asked if he wished to return to his earthly life. His immediate thought was "Return, of course not." But then he had a vision of his mother, and he said:

> …there's only one person really I want to go back for and that is my mum. I want to tell her that what she believes in is true, that there is a living God…'" God said to him, "If you return you must see things in a new light." From this, Ian understood that "I

must now see through his eyes, his eyes of love and forgiveness. I needed to see the world as he saw it— through the eyes of eternity.[28]

And that's when he returned.

It's highly relevant that Ian realised that he must learn to see through God's eyes of 'love and forgiveness'—those being the two pre-eminent features of God's nature that strike NDErs, as discussed in Chapters 11 and 12.

Rajiv Parti (Chapter 7) also learned during his NDE that he would receive divine guidance, but he had to choose whether or not to follow this guidance. His angelic helpers told him that they would give him guidance in how best to proceed in his life, but that this was just a road map that Rajiv himself had to take responsibility for following. From this, Rajiv realised that his life was not pre-ordained, and that he was free to make his own decisions.[13]

The Being of Light also told Rajiv that he must tap into the knowledge that he already possessed. The Being said: "Finding your own knowledge inside you is the best way to learn. If you don't learn for yourself, you will not learn completely."[13] This is echoed by the proposition I made in Chapter 9 that God has organised our time on Earth as a sort of 'problem-based learning' that works on exactly this principle—to learn completely requires learning for one's self. In other words, "…this life is a sort of 'training ground' in which being told too much too easily would be counter-productive for our education. We have to put in the effort—to face the challenges and solve the problems that bring us closer to God."[31]

We saw in Chapter 11 how the apostle Paul defined the qualities of love in his first letter to the Corinthians: amongst these, Paul stated that love *"does not insist on its own way"*[57]. In other words, love cannot demand or coerce.

In Chapter 12, we saw this demonstrated in Jesus' Parable of the Prodigal Son[69]. In that chapter, we concentrated on the unconditional love that the father showed for his wayward son on his return. But let's now think more about how the parable begins. The father didn't refuse the request of the younger son to be given his share of the property, and the father didn't try to prevent the son from then selling his property and going away to spend the money recklessly. In other words, the son was free to choose—although he made very bad choices which he later regretted!

Many Christians believe that the freedom of choice that we possess flows naturally from God's essential nature of unconditional love. Again, as Paul stated: love *"does not insist on its own way"*[57].

This is echoed by Howard Storm who, during his NDE, was told that "The ability to accept God's love or refuse it is the greatest freedom and the attribute God gives…God will not demand your love. That defeats the very nature of love. Love must be a choice. You cannot scare people into loving. That is not love, it is submission. God doesn't want slaves. God wants people freely to choose love."[29]

The theologian Thomas Jay Oord develops this theme by stating that God's love is not only unconditional, but is also uncontrolling. By this Oord means that God's love is "self-giving, others-empowering love."[87]

This concept is supported by numerous passages in the Bible and, in particular, by another of Paul's letters in the New Testament—in this case, his Letter to the Philippians, in which he writes:

> *Let each of you look not to your own interests, but to the interests of others. Let the same mind be in you that was in Christ Jesus, who, though he was in the form of God, did not regard equality with God as something to be exploited, **but emptied himself, taking the form of a slave**, being born in human likeness. And being found in human form, he humbled himself and became obedient to the point of death—even death on a cross.*[88]

Paul's letters were, of course, not originally written in English (a language which didn't exist 2,000 years ago!), but were written in Classical Greek. The rather strange phrase that's highlighted in the middle of this passage—"emptied himself"—is a translation of the Classical Greek word *kenosis.* There is no exact equivalent in English for the word *kenosis*, but Oord proposes that it encapsulates the concept of "self-giving, others-empowering love."[87]

We've said before that Jesus was essentially 'God in human form'. Indeed, as Jesus himself said, *"Whoever has seen me has seen the Father."*[89] Thus, "self-giving, others-empowering love" equally describes the nature of Jesus and of God.

But what does "self-giving, others-empowering love" actually mean? Well, part of the meaning, as mentioned above, is that God does not try to control obsessively or micro-manage Creation, like an authoritarian dictator would. Rather, God gives freedom and self-determination to Creation, and particularly to human beings. He doesn't want us to be like robots who are programmed only to do exactly what He would like us to do. God wants us to choose freely between living our lives as He hopes that we will, or to live our lives differently and distanced from God, if that's what we want to do.

No doubt you can see the parallels of this understanding of God's uncontrolling love with the choices put before the Israelites by Moses and Joshua, and Jesus' Parable of the Prodigal Son.

A helpful way of viewing this interaction between God and humanity (and Creation in general) is that it is 'open and relational.'[90] What this means is that God works with us through cooperation—it's a mutual relationship between

God and His Creation. In fact, I find it exciting to think of life as a collaborative adventure between God and ourselves! But, if we decide not to cooperate, God won't force us to do so—we are free to choose.

However, every choice we make has consequences—both for ourselves and for others. Paul puts this bluntly in his Letter to the Galatians: *"What a person plants, he will harvest. The person who plants selfishness, ignoring the needs of others—ignoring God!—harvests a crop of weeds. All he'll have to show for his life is weeds! But the one who plants in response to God, letting God's Spirit do the growth work in him, harvests a crop of real life, eternal life."*[91]

This is where the 'open' part of 'open and relational' comes into play. The future, which hasn't yet happened, is *not* already decided or fixed. Rather, it's 'open' to many possible outcomes—both good and bad. And it's our decisions—our choices—that are going to affect what the future looks like when it becomes the present. As we saw earlier in this chapter, this is what Rajiv Parti learned during his NDE: his future was not pre-determined—it was open to, and dependent on, the choices he made.[13]

Furthermore, what Ian McCormack, Howard Storm and Rajiv Parti learned during their NDEs was that our choices may have consequences not only during this life, but also for the life to come. If we deliberately choose separation from God during life on Earth, this may also feed through to the other side of death. God won't force us into Heaven! Fortunately, as Ian, Howard and Rajiv also discovered, God's love and forgiveness, that is available to all of us, continues in the spiritual dimension.

Another consequence of our freedom of choice is that our bad choices may not only cause suffering for ourselves, but also cause others to suffer. We've seen in Chapters 8 and 12 how many NDErs come to understand this during their 'life reviews'. So, in the next chapter, let's think about the topic that many find the most difficult to reconcile with the concept of a loving God—and that is suffering. Or, as C.S. Lewis described it, "The Problem of Pain."[92]

Things To Think About

FOR REFLECTION AND DISCUSSION

1) When you have an important choice to make, what sort of factors affect your decision?
2) Would your choices sometimes be different if you thought 'What would Jesus do?' or 'What would God want me to do?'?
3) Do you take freedom of choice for granted?
4) Are there times when you wish someone else would make a choice for you?

5) When Paul said in his letter to the Philippians that Jesus 'emptied himself, taking the form of a slave', how does this affect how you think about Jesus?

6) What do you think about the 'Open and Relational' view of how God interacts with Creation in general, with humans, and with you in particular?

7) Can God influence you to help you make the best choices? If so, how?

Chapter 15

Suffering

Many atheists—particularly those who've really thought about why they don't believe in God—would say that one of the main reasons is because of all the evil, pain and suffering in the World. "How," they would say, "could a benevolent, loving and merciful God permit the suffering that is all too apparent in the World? Or create a world in which such suffering is even possible?"

Well, it's a fair point, which needs an answer.

It's a question that some NDErs have posed.

This is what Crystal McVea said about her time in Heaven: "Alongside God, all the questions I had for Him no longer needed answers. How could He abide evil in this world?...In His presence, I knew in an instant that God's plan for us is perfect, even when bad things happen and we don't understand why."[30]

This echoes something that the Apostle Paul said in his first letter to the Corinthians: *"For now we see only a reflection as in a mirror; then we shall see face to face. Now I know in part; then I shall know fully, even as I am fully known."*[93]

It's indisputable that we have a very limited understanding of 'the mind of God'. How could it be otherwise, when our intellect is immeasurably smaller and more limited than God's, and our view of the true nature of reality is so narrow?

But while, during our Earthly lives, there's always going to be an element of 'playing the mystery card' when it comes to understanding suffering, it doesn't excuse us from striving to understand the best that we possibly can. Indeed, we've seen in previous chapters that part of our purpose in this life is to learn as much as we can about God while on Earth.

When, during his NDE, Howard Storm said that he couldn't return to the World because it's full of evil and ugliness, he was told, "The world has evil and ugliness in it, but there is also ample goodness, love, and beauty if you seek it."[29]

This is undoubtedly true. In fact, there are very good arguments, with data to support them, that there is a great deal more goodness, love and beauty in the World than there is evil, ugliness and suffering.[94] As we all know, we humans seem to have a morbid fascination with all the bad things that happen in the world, more so than the good— just look at the news any day of the week! This tends to skew our view of the true balance between goodness and badness in the world.

However, this still doesn't get round that fact that many very bad—indeed, completely evil—things happen that cause a great deal of suffering to both people and to Creation in general.

It's fair to say here that we are concerned with two main sources of suffering—that which is caused by nature and that which is caused by people.

In terms of natural causes of suffering, we're thinking of things like earthquakes, hurricanes, floods, infections, cancer, plus any other illnesses, diseases and natural disasters.

But then we have to ask why would a loving and benevolent God create a world (or even a universe) in which such causes of suffering to the inhabitants of that world are possible?

Well, perhaps part of the answer goes back to something discussed in chapter 3—the fine-tuning of the universe. As mentioned in that chapter, scientists now understand that the requirements for a universe to exist in which life is even possible, let alone can support highly complex life-forms like ourselves, are so stringent that even a slight deviation in any one of multiple properties (e.g. the strength of gravity) would abolish any possibility of life existing.

So, perhaps fine-tuning the universe to a level that is completely perfect *just for human beings* is impossible to achieve—even for God! Perhaps it's logically impossible, like asking God to create a married bachelor!

It was the German philosopher, Gottfried Leibniz, who famously proposed that perhaps we live in "the best of all possible worlds."[95] Put simply, his proposal is that perhaps a completely perfect world is impossible, but the one we inhabit is as near perfect as can ever be possible.

Take earthquakes, for example: these are caused when the tectonic plates of the Earth's crust rub against each other. So, if the Earth's crust was completely solid and there were no tectonic plates, there would be no earthquakes. However, scientists now understand that, if there were no tectonic plates, there would be very little or no life on Earth—certainly nothing as complex as us.[96] This is because the movements of these plates are essential for maintaining the Carbon Cycle, the Earth's temperature, and many other of the Earth's features that are essential for life. So, although earthquakes can be disastrous for those people who live where they occur, without earthquakes, there would be no people anywhere!

A similar argument can be made for illnesses and diseases. Like a finely-tuned sports car, our bodies are incredibly complicated and sophisticated machines—indeed, they are orders of magnitude more sophisticated and complicated than the most advanced sports car. But, just like mechanical machines, it's impossible to imagine a biological machine, like our bodies, that won't sometimes malfunction or be damaged or, indeed, will not eventually wear out.

In the case of cancer, for example, although the body has built in mechanisms to control the growth and proliferation of the cells that make up our bodies (and whose growth is essential to form our bodies), it's impossible to prevent every possible way in which a few cells might escape from these controls and become cancer cells.

Also with regard to infections: someone might ask, for example, why has COVID-19 happened? Well, there are about 200 different types of viruses that cause diseases in humans; but across the whole of nature there are *millions* of different types of viruses and it's estimated that less than 1% of these viruses actually cause diseases in animals or plants. Indeed, many viruses are actually beneficial. For example, there's a multitude of viruses that are naturally present in our bodies that actually protect us by infecting bacteria, and so keeping in check bacteria that might otherwise multiply out of control and themselves cause us problems and disease. Thus, like everything else in nature, there's a fine balancing act between benefit and detriment, and it's impossible for that always to be to the benefit of humans.

But let's now turn to that other type of suffering—that caused by humans themselves. This ranges from everyday thoughtless remarks that others may find hurtful, through to mental, physical or sexual abuse, and murder… and everything in between.

It's often stated that the possibility that humans can cause suffering to each other is an inevitable consequence of the freedom of choice that God gives to us, as discussed in the previous chapter.

Now this may seem fine in theory, but what about in practice? What about if you are the one who's been violently mugged, or whose family has been killed in a road traffic accident? How easy is it then to say, "Ah well, that's the price for our freedom of choice!"

Another argument some would make is to say that, in the above examples, God didn't cause the mugging or cause the traffic accident, but neither did He prevent these things from happening. So, surely a loving God would not allow such suffering to happen, if He could prevent it.

Let's imagine that someone witnessed the mugger attacking his victim, but did nothing and allowed the mugging to happen while thinking, "It would be wrong to intervene because that would compromise the free will of the mugger." Would you agree with that person's decision? Or would you actually think that person was guilty of not trying to help the victim when they might have done so?

So where does that leave us when we think about God and suffering? If God allows humans to cause suffering that He could prevent, can we say that God is loving?

Or, as some atheists would say, isn't that the best argument for believing that God doesn't exist?!

Thomas Jay Oord addresses this problem head on his book *God Can't* (and also in *The Uncontrolling Love of God*, which I referred to in Chapter 14).[97]

What Oord emphasises is that, although we accept that God is loving, we frequently (indeed, almost uniformly) under-estimate how much greater is God's love than anything of which we ourselves are capable or can fully comprehend. We looked at this in the previous chapter and considered the biblical basis for Oord's proposal that God's love can be defined as "self-giving, others-empowering" love. Not in the limited, wavering way of which we might be capable, but in a pure, perfect, unchanging and absolute form.

Oord then makes a further proposal that's particularly relevant to thinking about suffering. This is that God has *no choice* but *always and everywhere* to express this self-giving, others-empowering love. This is supported, again by words of the apostle Paul (in his letter to Timothy) when he states: *"If we are faithless, [God] remains faithful—for He cannot deny himself."*[98]

In other words, God cannot act other than according to His own nature of absolute love. To do so would be illogical and therefore as impossible as producing a round square!

Now, as we saw in Chapter 14, Paul tells us that love *"does not insist on its own way"*—it cannot coerce…it is "uncontrolling." So, God's perfect love is also, of necessity, uncontrolling. Oord proposes that the logical consequence of this is that God can't force his will on anyone or anything in Creation—He cannot coerce—He requires cooperation from within Creation for His will to be done.

A major conclusion of this approach is then to state not that 'God *causes* suffering', nor that 'God *allows* suffering', but that 'God *can't prevent* suffering *single-handedly*'.

So, this approach gives us a believable explanation for why suffering is present in the Creation of an All-Loving God—His perfect, unconditional and *uncontrolling* love cannot single-handedly override the freedom of choice which that love bestows.

The term 'single-handedly' used in the sentences above is not just an after-thought—it's integral to Oord's proposal that explains the occurrence of suffering within the Creation of a loving God. 'Single-handedly', in fact, takes us back to the 'open and relational' nature of the interactions between God and humanity discussed in Chapter 14.

God always works for good and always works against suffering, but absolutely needs *our* cooperation (as well as the cooperation of the rest of Creation) for His will to be done—for good to win.

Let's think back to the person who was witnessing the mugging. If that person was fully open to God's prompting—was in tune with God's will—then he or she wouldn't stand by, or turn the other way and do nothing to help the victim. It might be unwise and dangerous for the witness to intervene directly, but they might shout out and request help from others nearby, and immediately phone the police.

In a similar way, think back to the Parable of the Good Samaritan that we considered in Chapter 13. It was the Samaritan who, in relational response to God's wishes, did all he could to relieve the suffering of the victim of the mugging in that instance; rather than the priest or the Levite, who considered themselves holy and upright citizens but who were, in fact, much more concerned with their own sense of importance than they were with responding to God's wishes.

So, in summary, God never wants anyone to suffer. But suffering is inevitable so long as there are those who do not choose to accept, and live according to, God's unconditional and uncontrolling love.

Thomas Jay Oord develops this view of God's response to evil and suffering much further in his books *God Can't*[97]

and *God Can't: Questions and Answers.*[99] So, I recommend
these books if you'd like to read more about this.

Things To Think About
FOR REFLECTION AND DISCUSSION

---

1) Do you believe that suffering is an inevitable part
   of life?

2) When considering why there's suffering in the world,
   is it adequate to say 'It's a mystery, because God's
   ways are different from ours.'?

3) Do you agree that there is more good than evil in the
   world?

4) Should we blame God for 'natural disasters' and
   diseases?

5) What's your response to the statement that 'God
   can't prevent suffering singlehandedly'?

6) Do you struggle with the proposal that there are
   some things that God can't do?

7) If God does require our cooperation in order to
   prevent or limit suffering in the world, how much
   responsibility for the occurrence of suffering does
   that place on us?

8) Can prayer help to prevent or limit suffering?

Chapter 16

Faith

George Richie was only 20 years old when, in 1943, he died of double pneumonia in a military hospital in Texas.[100] For the rest of his life, he had the evidence that he had died that night in Camp Barkeley—this was in the form of his death certificate that had been signed by the clinician on duty at the time.

However, he was dead for only nine minutes, during which time he underwent an extremely vivid NDE.

During this experience, while next the bed where his dead body lay, George became aware of an impossibly bright light illuminating the room. As he later described it: "It was like a million welders' lamps all blazing at once."[100] Then, like other NDErs we've heard from in this book,

George realised that the light was a 'being'—in fact a man that he knew to be the Son of God, Jesus.

And, again, like the other NDErs' accounts we've considered, George knew with certainty that this 'being of light' also radiated an amazing, unconditional love. As George put it: "…I knew that this man loved me… what emanated from this presence was unconditional love. An astonishing love. A love beyond my wildest imagining."[100]

George then underwent a life review, with every scene from the 20 years of his life accompanied by the question: "What did you do with your life?"[100]

As George struggled to answer this question in a way that seemed adequate, Jesus reframed the question: "What have you done with your life to show Me?"[100]

Finally, realization hit George:

I had missed the point altogether. He was not asking about accomplishments and awards. The question, like everything else proceeding from Him, had to do with love. How much have you loved with your life? Have you loved others as I am loving you? Totally? Unconditionally? Hearing the question like that, I saw how foolish it was even to try to find an answer in the scenes around us. Why, I had not known love like this was possible. Someone should have told me, I thought indignantly! A fine time to discover what life was all about—like coming to a final exam and discovering you were going to be tested on a subject you had never studied. If this was the point of everything, why hadn't someone told me?[100]

Jesus answered George's question thus: "I did tell you...I told you by the life I lived. I told you by the death I died."[100]

George Ritchie went on to study medicine and became a psychiatrist. In 1965, he met Raymond Moody, whom he told about his experience in 1943, part of which is recounted above. It was this that prompted Moody, as mentioned in Chapter 5, to start collecting information from others who'd had similar experiences to Ritchie's, and led Moody to coin the term 'Near Death Experience.'[8]

There are two reasons why I've recounted parts of George Ritchie's NDE account in this chapter. One reason is that his account again emphasises that, as far as Jesus (and therefore, God) is concerned, the ultimate point of everything is love. And therefore, that is our purpose in life— to give and receive love.

The second reason is that George's experience answers the question, "How are we supposed to know that love is our purpose?" As Jesus told him: "I told you by the life I lived. I told you by the death I died."[100]

So why is it that so many people either don't believe this message, or choose to ignore it?

Well, that's where faith comes in.

In the Letter to the Hebrews in the New Testament, faith is defined thus: *"To have faith is to be sure of things hoped for, to be certain of things we cannot see."*[101] In other words, faith is believing something to be true that cannot be proven to everybody's satisfaction.

Everybody lives by faith.

An atheist believes that there is no God, but cannot prove it—it's a matter of faith.

A materialist believes that there is nothing to reality beyond the matter and energy of which our universe is composed, but cannot prove it—again, it's a matter of faith.

A Christian believes that there is a spiritual dimension to reality, that there is a God, and that Jesus is the Son of God (i.e. he lived on Earth as 'God in human form'). I've presented evidence in this book that's consistent with these beliefs. However, I have no doubt there are those who, if they read this book, will still say, "I don't believe it!" So, a Christian's beliefs, like everybody else's, remain a matter of faith.

Indeed, the desire of some *not* to believe there is a God was put quite bluntly by the philosopher Thomas Nagel when he wrote, "It isn't just that I don't believe in God and, naturally, hope that I'm right in my belief. It's that I hope there is no God! I don't want there to be a God; I don't want the universe to be like that."[102]

You may have heard someone being called a 'Doubting Thomas'. This term is used for someone who refuses to believe or accept something, even in the face of reasonable evidence. The original Thomas that's referred to here was one of the disciples of Jesus.

The first time that Jesus appeared to the group of disciples following his resurrection, Thomas was not there. What then transpired is recounted in John's Gospel:

One of the twelve disciples, Thomas (called the Twin), was not with them when Jesus came. So the other disciples told him, 'We have seen the Lord!' Thomas said to them, 'Unless I see the scars of the nails in his hands and put my finger on those scars and my hand in his side, I will not believe.' A week later the disciples were together again indoors, and Thomas was with them. The doors were locked, but Jesus came and stood among them and said, 'Peace be with you.' Then he said to Thomas, 'Put your finger here, and look at my hands; then reach out your hand and put it in my side. Stop your doubting, and believe!' Thomas answered him, 'My Lord and my God!' Jesus said to him, 'Do you believe because you see me? How happy are those who believe without seeing me!'[103]

So, Thomas finally believed that Jesus was alive again because he saw Jesus with his own eyes and, indeed, felt with his own hands the wounds still present from Jesus' execution and death.

But Jesus acknowledged the need of faith for belief by those who were not fortunate enough to be recipients of such incontrovertible evidence. Hence his words: *"How happy are those who believe without seeing me!"*[103]

Indeed, the Apostle Peter, who was one of the disciples present at both the appearances of the resurrected Jesus referred to above, wrote this about faith in Jesus in his first letter to fellow Christians: *"Although you have not seen him, you love him; and even though you do not see him now, you believe in him and rejoice with an indescribable and glorious joy, for you are receiving the outcome of your faith, the salvation of your souls."*[104]

Like Thomas, many NDErs return from their experience convinced of the reality of God and of his Son, Jesus Christ because of the evidence they have witnessed and experienced during their NDE. But whether others accept the truth of their testimonies is a matter of choice, and therefore a matter of faith. After all, as we discussed in Chapters 14 and 15, God's uncontrolling love ensures our freedom of choice!

Jesus actually illustrates this point in one of his parables. This is often referred to as the Parable of the Rich Man and Lazarus and is recounted in Luke's Gospel:

There was once a rich man who dressed in the most expensive clothes and lived in great luxury every day. There was also a poor man named Lazarus, covered with sores, who used to be brought to the rich man's door, hoping to eat the bits of food that fell from the rich man's table. Even the dogs would come and lick his sores. The poor man died and was carried by the angels to sit beside Abraham at the feast in heaven. The rich man died and was buried, and in Hades, where he was in great pain, he looked up and saw Abraham, far away, with Lazarus at his side... The rich man said, '... I beg you, father Abraham, send Lazarus to my father's house, where I have five brothers. Let him go and warn them so that they, at least, will not come to this place of pain.' Abraham said, 'Your brothers have Moses and the prophets to warn them; your brothers should listen to what they say.' The rich man answered, 'That is not enough, father Abraham! But if someone were to rise from death and go to them, then they would turn from their sins.' But Abraham said, 'If they will not listen to Moses and the prophets, they will not be convinced even if someone were to rise from death.' [105]

At one level, this parable can be seen as referring to Jesus' own death and resurrection—that some would not believe him to be the Son of God, even though he rose from the dead.

At another level, however, this parable is highly applicable to the contents of this book in that many NDErs can be likened to Lazarus, but *have* actually returned from the other side of death to tell us what it's all about—what the purpose of life really is!

It's also very relevant that many NDErs state that their transcendent experience of a Spiritual Dimension felt more real than the reality of life on Earth that we all experience. In his book *Through a Glass Darkly,* Alister McGrath discusses the analogy of reality, given by the classical Greek philosopher Plato, of prisoners trapped in a cave where they are chained facing the back wall of the cave.[106] For the prisoners, this is the only reality they can fully know. However, on the wall of the cave, they can see the shadows of people behind them moving about, and they catch echoes of the conversations between these people. But the prisoners' ability to understand this greater reality is hampered by their very limited and indirect access to it. Clearly, it's easy to apply this analogy to the prisoners' reality representing our material world and the greater reality of which they are dimly aware being the spiritual dimension.

McGrath goes on to discuss how Plato imagines one of the prisoners escaping from the cave, and who is then able to gain a much clearer and firmer understanding of the greater reality. This escapee then returns to the cave to tell the other prisoners about this. However, without having the first-hand experience themselves, the other prisoners struggle to comprehend fully what the escapee tells them. Indeed, one can easily imagine that some would simply respond, "I don't believe it!" This corresponds with Thomas' reaction when told about the visit of the resurrected Jesus, and the likely reaction of the Rich Man's relatives if faced with the spirit of Lazarus.

We could also suggest that NDErs are like Plato's escapee! They claim to have first-hand experience of the 'greater reality' of the Spiritual Dimension that most of us struggle either to sense or comprehend. But, like Plato's escapee, the NDErs have returned to tell us what they've discovered about the true nature of the spiritual reality.

Whether or not each one of us chooses to believe what these NDErs themselves are convinced of, is a matter of faith. Because, after all, we all have freedom of choice!

But perhaps, as Ian McCormack learned during his NDE, we should strive "to see... through the eyes of eternity."[28]

Things To Think About

FOR REFLECTION AND DISCUSSION

---

1) A survey in 2015 revealed that 40% of people in England do not believe that Jesus was a real person[107]. Why do you think this is the case?

2) How would you answer George Richie's question: "How are we supposed to know that love is our purpose[100]"?

3) Do you accept that what you believe about the 'nature of things' or your 'world view' is a matter of faith?

4) Why do you think that people like Thomas Nagel 'don't want there to be a God'?

5) If you had been the disciple Thomas, how would you have reacted when the other disciples said that they had seen the crucified Jesus alive?

6) In the Parable of the Rich Man and Lazarus, do you think Abraham was correct in saying that if people didn't believe the message of the Scriptures, neither would they believe even if someone rose from the dead?

7) Does the testimony of NDErs help to convince you that the Gospel message is true?

8) Do you find Plato's analogy of the 'prisoners in a cave' helpful in thinking about material reality versus spiritual reality?

9) Some Christians may struggle with, or not believe, that the testimony of NDErs is valid because they feel that NDEs are too far removed from traditional Christian understanding and beliefs. What do you think about this?

10) What do you think the NDEr Ian McCormack meant when he said he needed to learn 'to see through the eyes of eternity'?

Chapter 17

Soul

Why am I here?
Is there a point to it all?

What's the meaning of life?

These are the questions we started with in Chapter 1.

What we saw in Part 1 of this book is that, from a materialist or atheist perspective, there is no ultimate purpose to our life on Earth. And, once our body dies, everything for us comes to an end. Our 'being' is annihilated.

By contrast, we've seen that, if you accept that there *is* a spiritual dimension to reality, this completely changes the perspective on, and gives meaning to, your Earthly life. Because, when our body dies, our soul lives on in that spiritual dimension where, it seems, what we've done with our Earthly life is taken into account.

Even more so, if you accept that God does exist, and that God's pre-eminent nature is one of unconditional and uncontrolling love, our purpose then becomes clear.

This purpose is very simple to state, although perhaps more challenging for us to achieve—to love God, and to love each other, as God loves us.

In this way, our purpose is to promote well-being where ever and whenever we can.

Indeed, in *Pluriform Love,* Thomas Jay Oord points out that we often use the word 'love' without ever really defining what it means. And so, Oord gives the following very helpful definition: "To love is to act intentionally, in relational response to God and others, to promote overall well-being."[58]

Thus, we could also use this as the definition of our purpose in life: responding to a loving relationship with God by promoting the overall well-being of others.

What we've seen in this book is that many OBEs and NDEs provide evidence that is highly consistent with the existence of the spiritual dimension of reality, and also with the existence of God, whose nature is one of unconditional love and acceptance.

Furthermore, we've seen that much of the evidence from modern NDEs is highly consistent with the teachings in the Bible, and particularly with the New Testament that documents the life and teachings of Jesus Christ, and the response to Jesus of his early followers.

You'll note that, in the above two sentences, I use the words 'consistent with'—not 'proves' or even 'supports'—when talking about the evidence of OBEs and NDEs in relation to spiritual and religious beliefs.

This is because, as with most 'evidence', the information is open to different interpretations. For example, in chapter 3, we talked about the "fine-tuning of the universe." The evidence for this is rock solid. But what the evidence means is open to interpretation—some argue that it's evidence for the existence of a multi-verse whereas others argue that it's evidence for intelligent design of the universe (and is therefore consistent with belief in a Creator God).

This is why, as discussed in Chapter 16, a person's interpretation of the evidence of OBEs and NDEs is ultimately a matter of faith.

What I've shown through this book is that the reality of OBEs is strongly supported by the corroboration of OBE accounts by independent witnesses (e.g. medical staff present when the OBE happened), and the reality of NDEs is supported by their consistency between individuals and across cultures, visual NDEs in the blind, the life-changing effects on NDErs, and so on. This is why I believe these phenomena are telling us about the true nature of reality as expressed by Christianity and, indeed, other major religions, over many millennia.

One aspect of this is that, if one accepts that OBEs and NDEs provide insights into a spiritual reality, then they are consistent with the Christian belief that each of us has a soul that associates with our physical body during our life on Earth. The soul is then freed from the physical body when the latter dies, and lives on in the spiritual dimension.

By contrast, materialists think that our physical body is all that we are, so that when the body dies, we are no more.

Put in these terms, the Christian view of reality certainly seems the more positive and optimistic about the future that awaits each of us!

However, we can go a stage further with this by considering what philosophers call the idealist view: that 'spirit' is the true fundamental reality, and that material things are secondary to this. Keith Ward elegantly addresses this as follows:

...Materialists hold that everything that exists consists of matter. There are no spiritual realities, and matter probably consists of elementary particles governed by laws of nature. Those particles get into very complicated patterns, and when they are complicated enough they form human beings. Human consciousness, feeling, and thought are nothing but a complicated arrangement of material particles. Idealists, on the other hand, think that matter could not exist without mind or consciousness (what I have called Spirit). Material things exist, but they exist in order to express the nature of Spirit in some way. So Spirit is fundamentally real, and matter is dependent on Spirit.[108]

Angela Tilby pointed out that a theologian once said to her, "We don't *have* souls. We *are* souls."[109] In other words rather than thinking about each of us as being a physical body, and that we also happen to have a soul, we should think of this the other way round: each of us is first and foremost a soul, that has (or inhabits) a physical body while on Earth. The 'essential us' is our soul, not our body.

This is illustrated in the investigations of Peter Fenwick and Elizabeth Fenwick, who studied over 300 OBEs/ NDEs and published their findings in *The Truth in the Light*.[110] This is what they say about OBEs:

When people describe what it feels like to come out of their body and see themselves, they are in no doubt that the body they see is not the 'real me'. Whatever is real, whatever is true and vital for them is nothing to do with their physical body. That is simply the vehicle, as one person put it, for the real self… [One person said that she] was surprised 'how clearly I felt myself to be myself without my body'.[110]

Thought of like this, perhaps we should see every other person we encounter not so much as the physical body that we perceive with our physical senses, but rather as another immortal soul that happens to be inhabiting the body we see. Thus, every person—whether young or old, female or male, black or white, able-bodied or disabled, healthy or ill, fit or frail—is an immortal soul, loved and cherished by God. And what God wants is for us to see each other as He sees us, and therefore to love and cherish one another as He does.

As Ian McCormack learned during his NDE, he must "see through God's eyes of love and forgiveness."[28]

This is also how the Samaritan (described in the parable in Chapter 13) saw the injured Jew who'd been mugged on the road to Jericho.[83] He didn't see an enemy who despised him, but rather he saw a fellow human being—a 'poor soul'—who needed his love and care.

Indeed, as the Apostle Paul said when he spoke about God to the Greek philosophers in Athens, "…*in Him we live, and move and exist…We too are His children.*"[111]

And, as God's offspring, as Paul also wrote, we should "…clothe [our]selves with compassion, kindness, humility, gentleness, and patience...And to all these qualities add love, which binds all things together in perfect unity."[112]

God wants *you* to achieve this. That's why you are here.

Things To Think About
FOR REFLECTION AND DISCUSSION

---

1) Do you agree with Thomas Jay Oord's definition of love: "To love is to act intentionally, in relational response to God and others, to promote overall well-being."[58]?

2) How do you feel about the statement: "You don't have a soul. You are a soul."[109]?

3) To what extent is our reaction to, and relationship with, others determined by the 'person we see' rather than the 'person they are'?

4) How does the way we see other people differ from the way in which God sees them?

5) In the words of St Paul[112], to what extent do you clothe yourself with compassion, kindness, humility, gentleness, patience and, above all, love?

About the Author

Ian Todd, PhD, is a retired immunologist. He holds an honorary position at The University of Nottingham, where he was formerly Associate Professor and Reader in Cellular Immunopathology. He has over forty years' research experience in immunology and has contributed to over eighty peer-reviewed research publications. Ian has spent more than thirty years teaching immunology to medical, nursing and science students; he is a Fellow of the Higher Education Academy of the United Kingdom. He is a co-author of the text book *Lecture Notes: Immunology* (Seventh Edition, Wiley-Blackwell, Chichester/Oxford, 2015).

Ian was, for many years, a member of the Methodist Church in Britain. He now attends the Anglican Church of St Mary the Virgin in Wirksworth, Derbyshire, UK, where he has served as Churchwarden. Ian has particular interests in Open and Relational Theology and the interface of science and religion. Some of his writings in these areas are available at: iantodd2.wixsite.com. Ian is a 'voice' at the Center for Open and Relational Theology.

Ian lives in Wirksworth, England, with his wife, Sue.

Endnotes

1. Seth, Anil. *Being You: A New Science of Consciousness.* Faber and Faber, 2021.
2. Dawkins, Richard. *River Out of Eden: A Darwinian View of Life.* Weidenfeld and Nicolson, 2014.
3. Bruce, Steve. *British Gods: Religion in Modern Britain.* Oxford University Press, 2020.
4. Miller, J. Steve. *Faith That's Not Blind: A Brief Introduction to Contemporary Arguments for the Existence of God.* Wisdom Creek Academic, 2016.
5. Epstein, Robert. "Brain as Transducer: What if the brain is not a self-contained information processor? What if it is simply a transducer?" *ScienceOpen Preprints* 1 (2021).
6. Nahm, Michael, Bruce Greyson, Emily Williams Kelley, and Erlendur Haraldsson. "Terminal Lucidity: A Review and a Case Collection." *Archives in Gerontology and Geriatrics* 55, no. 1 (2012): 138-42.
7. Haig, Scott. "The Brain: The Power of Hope." *Time Magazine* 169 (2007): 118–19.
8. Moody, Raymond. *Life After Life.* 25ᵗʰ Anniversary Edition. Rider, 2001
9. van Lommel, Pim, Ruud van Wees, Vincent Meyers, and Ingrid Elfferich. "Near-Death Experience in Survivors of

Cardiac Arrest: A Prospective Study in the Netherlands."
In *Lancet* 358 (2001): 2039-45.

10. Sabom, Michael. *Recollections of Death.* Corgi, 1982.

11. Sabom, Michael. *Light and Death: One Doctor's Fascinating Account of Near-Death Experiences.* Zondervan, 2011.

12. Sartori, Penny. *The Near Death Experiences of Hospitalized Intensive Care Patients: A Five-Year Clinical Study.* The Edwin Mellen Press, 2008.

13. Parti, Rajiv, and Paul Perrry. *Dying to Wake Up.* Hay House, 2016.

14. Greyson, Bruce. *After: A Doctor Explores What Near Death Experiences Reveal About Life and Beyond.* Transworld Digital, 2021.

15. Long, Jeffrey, and Paul Perry. *Evidence of the Afterlife: The Science of Near-Death Experiences.* Harper Collins Publishers, Inc., 2011.

16. Parnia, Sam, Stephen G. Post, and Matthew T. Lee, et al. "Guidelines and standards for the study of death and recalled experiences of death—a multidisciplinary consensus statement and proposed future directions." *Annals of the New York Academy of Sciences* (2022).

17. Long, Jeffrey. "Near-Death Experiences: Evidence for Their Reality." *Missouri Medicine* 111, no. 5 (2014): 372-80.

18. Ring, Kenneth, and Sharon Cooper. "Near-Death and Out-of-Body Experiences in the Blind. A Study of Apparent Eyeless Vision." *Journal of Near Death Experiences* 16, no. 2 (1997): 101-47.

19. Ring, Kenneth, and Sharon Cooper. *Mindsight: Near-Death Experiences and Out-of-Body Experiences in the Blind.* iUniverse, 2008.

20. Miller, J. Steve. *Near-Death Experiences as Evidence for the Existence of God and Heaven: A Brief Introduction in Plain Language.* Wisdom Creek Press, 2012.

21. Carter, Chris. *Science and the Near-Death Experience: How Consciousness Survives Death.* Inner Traditions, 2010.

22. Sartori, Penny. *Wisdom of Near-Death Experiences: How Understanding NDEs Can Help Us Live More Fully.* Watkins Publishing, 2014.

23. Greyson, Bruce, Emily Williams Kelly, and Edward Kelly. "Explanatory Models of Near-Death Experiences." In *The Handbook of Near-Death Experiences: Thirty Years of Investigation.* Edited by Janice Miner Holden, Bruce Greyson, and Debbie James. Praeger Publishers, 2009.

24. Habib, Samaa, and Bodie Thoene. *Face to Face with Jesus.* Chosen Books, 2014.

25. Burke, John, and Kathy Burke. *Imagine Heaven Devotional: 110 Reflections to Bring Heaven to Your Life Today.* Baker Book, 2018.

26. Bush, Nancy Evans. "Distressing Western Near-Death Experiences: Finding a Way Through the Abyss." In *The Handbook of Near-Death Experiences: Thirty Years of Investigation.* Edited by Janice Miner Holden, Bruce Greyson, and Debbie James. Praeger Publishers, 2009.

27. Burke, John. *Imagine Heaven: Near-Death Experiences, God's Promises, and the Exhilarating Future That Awaits You.* Baker Books, 2015.

28. Sharkey, Jenny. *Clinically Dead: I've seen Heaven and Hell.* CreateSpace Independent Publishing, 2012.

29. Storm, Howard. *My Descent into Death: and the Message of Love Which Brought Me Back.* Clairview Books, 2012.

30. McVea, Crystal, and Alex Tresniowski. *Waking Up in Heaven: A True Story of Brokenness, Heaven and Life Again.* Howard Books, 2013.

31. Todd, Ian. "Partnering With the Perfect Educator." In *Partnering With God: Exploring Collaboration in Open and Relational Theology.* Edited by Tim Reddish, Bonnie Rambob, Fran Stedman, and Thomas Jay Oord. SacraSage Press, 2021.

32. Lewis, C.S. *Surprised By Joy: The Shape of My Early Life.* William Collins, 2010 (1955).

33. Neal, Mary. *To Heaven and Back: A Doctor's Extraordinary Account of Her Death, Heaven, Angels and Life Again.* WaterBrook Press, 2011.

34. 2 Corinthians 12:1-5 (The Message).

35. Acts of the Apostles 14:19-20 (The Message).

36. Roth, Sid, and Lonnie Lane. *Heaven is Beyond Your Wildest Expectations: The True Stories of Experiencing Heaven.* Destiny Image, 2012.

37. Black, Dale, and Ken Gire. *Flight to Heaven: A Plane Crash…A Lone Survivor…A Journey to Heaven—and Back.* Bethany House Publishers, 2010.

38. Genesis 1:1-4 (New Revised Standard Version (NRSV)).

39. Psalms 18:28 (Good News Translation (GNT)).

40. Psalms 27:1 (GNT).

41. Isaiah 9:2 (GNT).

42. Matthew 4:16. (GNT).

43. John 8:12 (NRSV).

44. 1 John 1:5-7 (The Message).

45. Matthew 17:1-3 (GNT).

46. 1 Peter 2:9 (GNT).

47. Matthew 5:14-16 (GNT).

48. Lennon, John, and Paul McCartney. "All You Need is Love." Capitol Records, 1967.

49. 1 John 4:16. (New International Version (NIV)).

50. Oord, Thomas Jay. *Open and Relational Theology: An Introduction to Life Changing Ideas.* SacraSage Press, 2021.

51. Deuteronomy 7:9 (GNT).

52. Psalms 63:3 (GNT).

53. Psalms 86:15 (GNT).

54. Jeremiah 31:3 (The Message).

55. John 3:16. (GNT).

56. John 15:12 (GNT).

57. 1 Corinthians 13:4-8a (English Standard Version).

58. Oord, Thomas Jay. *Pluriform Love.* SacraSage Press, 2022.

59. Romans 8:38-39 (NRSV).

60. 1 John 4:8 (NIV).

61. Luke 23:34 (GNT).

62. John 19:30 (GNT).

63. Luke 8:49-56 (GNT).

64. John 11:1-44 (GNT).

65. Colossians 2:13-14 (The Message).

66. Psalms 85:5 (NIV).

67. Colossians 1:13-14 (GNT).

68. 1 John 1:9 (GNT).

69. Luke 15:11-24 (GNT).

70. Acts of the Apostles 17:26-27 (GNT).

71. Ephesians 5:1 (GNT).

72. Ephesians 5:2a (GNT).

73. John 13:34-35 (GNT).

74. Reynolds, Malvina. "Love is Something (Magic Penny)." Track 12 *Sings the Truth*. Northern Music Corporation, 1967.

75. Matthew 7:12 (GNT).

76. James 2:8 (The Message).

77. The Prophet Muhammed, Hadith.

78. Mahabharata 5:1517.

79. Udana-Varga 5.18.

80. T'ai Shang Kan Ying P'ien 213-218.

81. Matthew 5:43-48 (GNT).

82. Matthew 18:21-22 (GNT).

83. Luke 10:25-37 (GNT).

84. "Names of people mentioned most often in the Bible." Southern Nazarene University. http://home.snu.edu/~hculbert/wordsr.htm

85. Deuteronomy 30:19-20 (GNT).

86. Joshua 24:14-15 (GNT).

87. Oord, Thomas Jay. *The Uncontrolling Love of God.* InterVarsity Press, 2016.

88. Philippians 4:2-8 (NRSV).

89. John 14:9 (NRSV).

90. Oord, Thomas Jay. *Open and Relational Theology: An Introduction to Life-Changing Ideas.* SacraSage Press, 2021.

91. Galatians 6:7b-8 (The Message).

92. Lewis, C.S. *The Problem of Pain.* The Centenary Press, 1940.

93. 1 Corinthians 13:12 (NIV).

94. Bregman, Rutger. *Human Kind: A Hopeful History.* Bloomsbury Publishing, 2019.

95. Antognazza, Maria Rosa. *Leibniz: A Very Short Introduction.* Oxford University Press, 2016.

96. Boyle, Rebecca. "Why Earth's Cracked Crust May be Essential for Life." *Quanta Magazine* (June 17, 2018).

97. Oord, Thomas Jay. *God Can't.* SacraSage Press, 2019.

98. 1 Timothy 2:13 (NRSV).

99. Oord, Thomas Jay. *God Can't: Questions and Answers.* SacraSage Press, 2020.

100. Ritchie, George G., and Elizabeth Sherrill. *Return from Tomorrow.* Chosen Books, 2007.

101. Hebrews 11:1 (GNT).

102. Nagel, Thomas. *The Last Word.* Oxford University Press, 1997.

103. John 20: 24-29 (GNT).

104. 1 Peter 1: 8-9 (NRSV).

105. Luke 16: 19-31 (GNT).

106. McGrath, Alister. *Through a Glass Darkly: Journeys through Science, Faith and Doubt.* Hodder & Stoughton, 2020.

107. "2019 Research from the Course." *Talking Jesus.* Talkingjesus.org.

108. Ward, Keith. *The Evidence for God: The Case for the Existence of the Spiritual Dimension.* Darton, Longman and Todd, 2014.

109. Tilby, Angela. "'Identity' is a worrying obsession." *Church Times* no. 8293, (February 25, 2022): 15.

110. Fenwick, Peter, and Elizabeth Fenwick. *The Truth in the Light.* White Crow Books, 1996.

111. Acts of the Apostles 17:28 (GNT).

112. Colossians 3:12b, 14 (GNT).

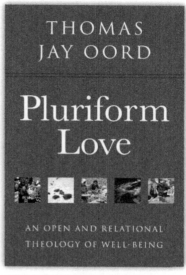
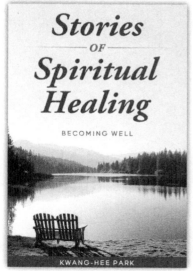
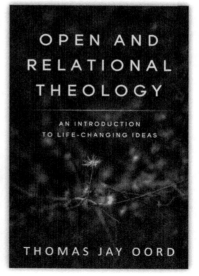

Printed in Great Britain
by Amazon